C000174802

This book is for you if

- you have ever wondered what ⸗
  i.e. 'Gentle Jesus meek and mil

- you enjoy historical novels;

- you would like to experience Jesus without 1900 years of church tradition;

- you are interested in walking with Jesus day by day during Holy Week;

- you are curious about the Jewish worship and prayer that Jesus took part in in his last days on earth;

- you want to get new insights into the actual historical events of the last eight days of Jesus' life, i.e. on Palm Sunday why did he arrive at the Temple late?

What they say

Novel, textbook, journal and devotional - Andy Roland's 'exercise in historical imagination' is hard to categorise. The main section of the book is a narrative account of Jesus' last eight days, written as fiction but still faithful to the Gospel accounts.... If Roland's desire is to bring the story of Jesus alive to a new audience and answer questions about the cultural context then the book succeeds.

Premier Christianity, May 2021

Well! Holy Week has come alive in a new way and will never be the same again. The book has finally removed set images and confusions stuck in my mind from so many years and something much more vibrant and alive has replaced them. I especially appreciated the trial scenes and the final hours of Jesus life. Just a couple of things I found distracting. Sometimes scholarship drew me away from the pace of the narrative, and I did not like the name of 'trainees' for the twelve disciples. I also found using the Aramaic names a nuisance!

Sr Hilda Mary CSC, St Michael's Convent

I much enjoyed reading Jesus the Troublemaker during Holy Week. It seeks to place readers back into the world of 1st century Jewish Jerusalem, behind the tradition as it were. There are times when imagination has been needed to plug the gaps; but I think that is done persuasively.

Rt Revd Michael Ipgrave, Bishop of Lichfield,
author of 'Scriptures in Dialogue - the Bible and the Qur'an'

An interesting and challenging book.

Rabbi Helen Freeman, West London Synagogue

This is an imaginative portrayal of the last week of Jesus' life, and of subsequent events. It is based on the accounts in the gospels, but incorporates the author's linguistic, historical, geographical and architectural knowledge of Jerusalem and the surrounding area. Jesus is referred to mostly by his Hebrew name Yeshua, except in one chapter when the Greek Iēsous is also used. I liked in particular the description of Jewish customs such as the Hebrew blessings for bread and wine that were used at the Last Supper. His description of the trials of Jesus before the Sanhedrin, Herod and Pilate are vivid, and his description of the flogging and the crucifixion are chilling. The account of the first resurrection appearances were a joy to read. The difficulty of identifying the exact location of the trials before Pilate and Herod are sensibly dealt with in endnotes rather than the main body of the text. His portrayal of Caiaphas is handled sympathetically, rather than portraying him as an out-and out rogue. I loved it.

James Behrens, barrister, author of 'Practical Church Management'

JESUS
THE TROUBLEMAKER

HIS LAST 8 DAYS

The Drama of Holy Week Reimagined

REV ANDY ROLAND

Published by Filament Publishing Ltd
16, Croydon Road, Waddon, Croydon, Surrey CR0 4PA

The right of Andrew Roland to be identified as the author of this
work has been asserted by him in accordance with
the Design and Copyright Act 1988

Printed by 4Edge

ISBN 978-1-913623-40-1

Contents

List of illustrations

Maps

Illustrations

1. Information for Visitors from Mars

The Roman Empire
Two thousand years ago in Earth time, the whole of southern
Europe and North Africa were joined together in a Mediterranean-
wide customs union we call the Roman Empire. The small city
state of Rome in Italy had conquered all this territory. Fifty years
earlier it had become a military autocracy, and was now ruled by a
succession of Caesars or emperors in Italy, with soldiers stationed
everywhere. Although the Romans spoke Latin, the universal
language of the empire was Greek, building on the centuries of
trading that the Greek city states had been involved in. The glue
that kept the empire together was a tolerant attitude towards the
various religions in different lands, whether people sacrificed to
Jupiter, or Zeus, or Artemis or Isis or whoever.

Judaea
At the eastern end of the empire was a different kind of country
called Judaea. It had been ruled for thirty years by a half-Jewish
king, Herod, who had been appointed by Caesar. At the time this
book is set, it was split into four parts: Judaea together with
Samaria were ruled by a Roman governor and the three other
parts were ruled by descendants of Herod.

Unlike the rest of the known world, this people, the Jews, had no
statues or images in their worship. They believed in one supreme
God who was beyond all human categories. The focus of their
religion was a magnificent temple in Jerusalem, built by King
Herod, where they sacrificed animals as a regular part of worship.
Jews lived not only in Judaea but all over the empire. There were
probably about a million Jews living in Judaea and Galilee, roughly
the same number as lived in Egypt. The highest authority in Israel
was the High Priest in Jerusalem and the Council of Elders called
the Sanhedrin.

Galilee

Five days' walk north from Jerusalem was the district of Galilee, ruled by Herod Antipas. In the middle was a major city called Sepphoris, built in the best Greek style. Five miles from there was a small village called Nazareth. In it was a carpenter and stone mason called Yeshua, known to the world now as Jesus, the Greek form of his name. About 25 years after Rome had taken control of Judaea and Jerusalem, Jesus started a preaching and healing ministry, wandering around small towns and villages of Galilee. He became very popular and was widely regarded as a prophet. Our story opens about three years later when he and his followers were on their road to the Temple in Jerusalem to celebrate the most important festival of the Jewish year, the Passover.

Today

Those who look to Jesus as their spiritual leader today numbered 2,380,000,000 or 31% of the global population (2015 figures). So what was Jesus actually like? 'Jesus The Troublemaker' aims to give a living portrait of the man whose life, death and rising again has so dramatically influenced the world.

2. Questions, questions, questions

What are the sources?

The story of 'The Troublemaker' is based on four ancient accounts in the Bible, detailing the ministry of Jesus. They are the gospels of Matthew, Mark, Luke and John. It is remarkable how detailed the accounts are for the last week of Jesus' life. It makes it possible to write a novel about Jesus' last days which stays close to the recorded events. I set out how and why I have used these sources in 'Examining the Gospels' on page 193.

I have used my imagination to recreate the words and conversations of Jesus, much in the style of a film script. In every section I have indicated the gospel passage which lies behind it, and have explained some the background to the stories.

Writing it has been a fascinating and educational journey. The discipline of writing a novel is more exacting than writing a devotional. Where there are differences between the various gospels, I had to make a choice and give reasons for my choice. I also needed to work out the details of place and time, and fill in those instances about which the gospels are silent, e.g. how did the disciples get the lamb for the Passover supper?

Near the end I describe how I came to write the book, and the challenges of creating some sort of historical novel. This is in 'The Story of the Book' on page 185.

How Jewish was Jesus?
I have tried to place Jesus fully into his Jewish context, using Hebrew or Aramaic versions of the names in the story, as well as all the names for God. Jesus' home language was Aramaic. He knew enough Hebrew to read the Jewish Scriptures, which he called 'the Law and the Prophets'. He also probably spoke some Greek. I go into the language question in more detail in 'Languages and Names', on page 207.

There is a thematic glossary of Hebrew, Aramaic and English words from page 235.

Where can I read about the politics and religion of Judaea?
A more detailed discussion of the religious and political background is provided in 'History and Politics' on page 213, and in 'Religion and Division', on page 223.

Now read on

You don't need to bother with any of the detailed background information to enjoy the story and the dramatic encounters Jesus had with people. The notes and information at the back are there as a resource for the curious. But if you want to learn more about any particular aspect of the story, Wikipedia is a wonderful resource!

Judaea, Samaria and Galilee at the time of Jesus

8th Nisan

Six days before Passover

Jericho - Zacchaeus

Note: Nisan is the first month of the Jewish religious year roughly equating to April.

The fields of Jericho with the Wilderness of Judaea or Mount of Temptation behind

The Pilgrimage Trail[1, 2]

It was hot in the Jordan valley. It was mid-March, less than a month since there had been snow in Yerushalayim. But the Jordan valley is 850 feet below sea level and has its own micro-climate. The fast-flowing river added humidity to the heat of the sun, with lush patches of jungle interspersed by banana, date and lemon groves.

The broad path along the west bank of the Jordan normally saw just a handful of farmers with donkeys and wagons, and an occasional rich man's chariot. Roman legionaries were scarce, being based at important cities like Caesarea, Samaria, and Yerushalyim. This morning, however, the flat path was being used by literally thousands of people, all walking in the same direction. They were religious Jews, almost all from the northern, 'Gentile Region' (Galil ha-Goyim)[3]. This had been conquered and converted to Judaism in the great Maccabean Revolt, less than two hundred years before. Being new converts, Galileans were fervent, emotional and a long way from the Temple priests in Yerushalayim. They avoided walking through the heretical region of Samaria, even though it meant making a detour of over thirty miles, another two days walking in the Jordan heat, another two nights wrapped up in their cloaks in the chilly night air.

On they came, thousands of families, men, women and children, accompanied by the obligatory sheep. Many were walking

17

quite purposefully, for they only had a couple of days to reach Yerushalayim. People had been streaming along the valley for the past two days, and there were now plenty who resigned themselves to arriving late.

Among them was a couple of hundred of Galileans, men and women and a few children, who were looking not merely anxious but scared. In stark contrast to the festive and expectant atmosphere of the other pilgrim groups. Slightly ahead of them were a dozen burly bearded men, Rabbi Yeshua's trainees[5], looking bewildered as if they were not sure what was around the next corner. And ahead of them, a solitary figure, striding fast, his body tense and his face set, Yeshua from Natzeret, the prophet from the Galil.

After walking a couple of hours, Yeshua gave the nod for people to have a rest. The twelve sat down around him, keeping an eye out for any possible hostiles they might need to defend their rabbi from.

"Listen!" said Yeshua. *"we are going up to Yerushalayim, and the Son of Man will be handed over to the leading priests and the Torah-teachers[4], and they will condemn him to death; then they will hand him over to the Goyim; they will mock him, and spit upon him, and flog him, and kill him; and after three days he will rise again."*

The group sat stunned, mouths open, hardly able to move. There was a full two minutes' silence. Then Yeshua stretched his back, got up and said, *"Time to get moving."* The twelve got up too and followed him, still with shocked expressions on their faces.

Two hours later they had another break. Two of the group, clearly brothers, asked in a low, somewhat embarrassed voice, if they could talk to him beyond the group's hearing. They moved a few yards away.

"So, what do my two thunder-lads[6] want?"

Ya'akov, the elder, spoke. *"Rabbi, we want you to say yes to the favour we're going to ask."*

A light smile came to Yeshua's face. *"That sounds like a serious ask. What is it?"*

"When you come to reign as king, can I be your right-hand man? Can Yochanan and I be your two chief ministers?"

Yeshua drew a deep breath and looked steadily from one to the other. They shifted uneasily as they tried and failed to meet his direct gaze. He said, *"You haven't a clue what you're asking. Can you pass the test I will be taking? Or can you sign up for the same struggle?"*

"Yes, Rabbi, I'm sure we can!"

"Well, you will undergo the same test as I will, and you will sign up for the same struggle, but as for being my two right-hand men, I'm not in control of that. I can't make any promises."

Mumbling apologetically the two crest-fallen brothers returned to the group. Yeshua sat for some minutes, lost in thought. He was roused by angry voices coming from the twelve.

"I can't believe that you had the brass neck!"

"What chutzpah!"

"We really know who our friends are now, don't we!"

Yeshua quickly rejoined his trainees[5]. *"Settle down, lads, settle down. You've got it all wrong. Listen, you know that anyone who wants to climb the greasy pole in Herod's court or in Pilate's palace, they're self-important, they expect everyone to kow-tow to them and they collect people to look up at them as their patrons. It won't be like that with you. Here anyone who wants to be important must do* the washing up. In my world, the way of getting to the top is to stay at the bottom. Even I didn't come to have people do things for me. I came to do things for them. Come on lads, let's get going. It isn't too far to Yericho. That's where we'll stay."

Jericho[7]

As the pilgrims approached Yericho[8], the countryside became a flat rocky desert, and they were relieved to see the green of the palm trees on the near horizon, overlooked by Herod's castle. After a few miles of plantations, Yeshua and his followers reached the village in front of the town of Yericho proper, with its large villas for Yerushalayim temple staff and local aristocracy. The village he approached housed workers on the nearby date palm plantations. A young lad approached them and asked who they were.

"We're followers of Yeshua the prophet," he was told. The boy sped back to the village and soon a crowd of women, men and children had gathered, shouting a welcome. Yeshua smiled broadly and put his hand on the heads of the children who approached:
"Barukh ata Adonai Eloheynu, melekh ha'olam[9], who has created these your children as a blessing and to be a blessing." For the first time for hours, he relaxed.

As they made their way between the square whitewashed houses and their security walls, the street filled with yet more villagers. Then, in the distance, almost where the large two-storey stone villas could be seen, Yeshua stopped and looked curiously at a tree two hundred paces away.

He leant towards an elderly man near him and asked, "Who's the man up that tree?"

The man looked up and his mouth dropped open in surprise. With a grimace he said, "I can't believe it. That's - that's Zakkai![10] What's he doing in our part of town? And up a tree, in the name of Elaha[11]!"

"And just who is Zakkai?"

"Only the head of the tax farmers in the region.[12] And, by Elaha, doesn't he farm the taxes well. He's a swindler, an extortioner, a miser and a Roman toady. He's got half our town in debt to pay for his rake-off. His name Zakkai - Righteous - what a joke! And now, unbelievably, he's climbing a tree! Doesn't he have any dignity?"

"I can see why he's unpopular," said Yeshua thoughtfully. *"But still,"* he smiled disconcertingly, *"he does climb trees."*

A couple of minutes later they reached the spot where Zakkai in an incongruously ornate cloak was clinging to a branch, trying to look as if he wasn't there. A few of the braver elements of the crowd spat in his direction.

Yeshua stopped and called out, *"Zakkai!"*

The little man almost fell off the branch with shock. *"Zakkai, you'd better shin down. I'm staying at your place this weekend!"*

The adoring crowd quickly changed their tune. *"Unbelievable!"* *"Is he a real prophet?"* *"You can't trust Galileans."* *"What a fake!"*. Yeshua just stood there amid the turmoil, waiting while Zakkai tumbled down the tree. He stood in front of Yeshua, twigs and leaf dust in his hair and on his torn robe. Open-mouthed, trying to gather his wits.

"R-rabbi - you're coming to my house? Really?"

"If you'll have me."

"Rabbi - I don't know what to say. I've not lived well." He gathered his wits. *"Listen, tell you what I'll do. I'm going to give half of my possessions to people on the breadline. And if I've cheated anyone -"* the crowd murmured, 'Who haven't you?' - *"anyway, I'll pay them back not double but four times over!"*

The crowd stood in stunned silence for a moment, then shouts erupted, *"Good ol' Zak !" "Blessings on you, Zakkai!" "Three cheers for Zak!"*

Yeshua looked round grinning, then shouted, *"Today - today - salvation has come to this man! This son of Abraham. This fellow Jew! This righteous man! Come on, Zakkai, lead the way."*

The whole delighted crowd followed Yeshua and Zakkai out of the village to a large ornate villa, none happier than Yeshua's twelve trainees, looking forward to their first comfortable night's sleep for five days.

Notes for 8th Nisan/Friday

[1] The source is Mark 10.32-45

[2] Passover always fell on the 14th Nisan, at the full moon. The Jewish calendar was lunar, and so had 13 months in the year, with an extra month every five years. The Hebrew word is *Pesach*.

[3] Isaiah 9.1, written about 620 BCE, says, *'In the former time he brought into contempt the land of Zebulun and the land of Naphtali, but in the latter time he will make glorious the way of the sea, the land beyond the Jordan, Galilee of the nations.'* Or *'Galilee of the Gentiles'* - *Galil Goyim*.

[4] I have used the term 'leading priests' instead of 'chief priests' to give the idea of the hereditary and aristocratic status of the priests. They were at the top of the Jerusalem hierarchy.

In 'The Jewish New Testament' David H Stern used the phrase 'Torah-teachers' for 'scribe'. Scribe is the literal translation of the Greek word, but the actual activity of these men was teaching and was central to the religious life of the people.

[5] Disciples is rather a churchy word. The Hebrew word *talmidim* means more than just being educated. It primarily meant taking on the whole way of life exemplified by one's teacher. I have taken 'trainee' as the nearest in meaning, short for trainee missionaries or trainee church founders.

[6] Ya'akov and Yochanan were given the nickname 'sons of thunder' by Yeshua because of their hot tempers, an example is in Luke 9.52-55: *'(Jesus' messengers) entered a village of the Samaritans to make ready for him; but they did not receive him, because his face was set towards Jerusalem. When his disciples James and John saw it, they said, 'Lord, do you want us to command fire to come down from heaven and consume them?' But he turned and rebuked them.' (NRSV)*

[7] The source is Luke 19.1-9. The final verse has been placed in Jesus' talk in the synagogue on the following day.

[8] Yericho, or Jericho, was a major city in Jesus' day. King Herod had built three palaces there and brought more water in via an aqueduct. Dates were a major industry. After the Jewish revolt 66-70 it declined to a small Roman garrison town.

[9] "Blessed are you, Lord our God, King of the universe," is the standard opening of innumerable Jewish prayers.

[10] 'Zakkai' is the Hebrew form of the Greek 'Zacchaeus'

[11] 'Elaha' is the Aramaic word for God. And Jesus spoke Aramaic. It is used in those parts of the Old Testament, (the Law & the Prophets or the Tenakh), which are in Aramaic, viz. parts of Ezra and Daniel in the Old Testament.

[12] Tax farming was how the Roman empire got its revenues. Periodically, the administration would put up for auction the right to collect taxes in various regions. The one who contracted to get the largest amount won, and he then had to get his own rake-off. It was a system not so much open to corruption as reliant on corruption.

SATURDAY/SABBATH

9th Nisan

Five days before Passover

Jericho - the Synagogue[1]

Reconstructed synagogue in Nazareth village

The synagogue was crowded. Apart from the normal local congregation, Zakkai was there, with an apparently permanent look of surprise on his face. Yeshua had brought along his twelve trainees, together with his mother and several of his women followers, all wearing quality clothes. They obviously had their own means of support, and indeed were key funders of Yeshua's ministry.

After the reading of the Torah and Haftorah (the Law and the Prophets), the synagogue leader sent Yeshua a message, saying, *"Rabbi, if you have any word of exhortation for the people, please give it."* Yeshua went to the front and sat down on the teaching seat. A rapt hush fell on the congregation.

"My brothers and sisters, I guess you're still asking yourselves about my meeting up yesterday with my good friend Zakkai." A murmur of mixed approval and disapproval ran round the hall. *"Let me ask you a question. When do you ask the doctor to come and see you? When you're well, or when you're ill? You know the answer to that. Well, that's just why I've come. I, son of man[2], have come to look for and to liberate the lost.*

"Let me tell you a story. A man had two teenage sons - and you know what teenagers are like. One midsummer, the man organised his servants for the grape harvest. He asked his two boys to help and so speed things up. One said, 'Oh, give me a break.' The other said, 'I'll go right now!' But in fact the first, grumbling a bit, took off his house

clothes and worked alongside his father's servants. The second son did nothing. Now - which one did what his father wanted?"

"The first one," shouted some of the congregation.

"Exactly," said Yeshua. *"You all knew Yochanan - he baptised just a few miles from here. And who embraced his message of having to make a new start? Was it the priests? The learned rabbis? Or was it the tax farmers and escorts? The ones everyone despised? They knew they had to wipe the slate clean with God. That's why, in the economy of heaven, the last shall be first and the first last."*

Yeshua stood up and resumed his place in the middle of the congregation. The excited buzz that arose stopped as the synagogue leader started intoning the prayers, but started up again as the service ended and everyone went back home for the Shabbat lunch.

For the remainder of the day, apart from the early evening meal, they rested, in obedience to the commandment.[3,4]

Notes for 9th Nisan/Shabbat (Saturday/Sabbath)

[1]This section is entirely my own invention. We have no record of what happened on the Sabbath/Saturday, except we can assume that Yeshua and his trainees would have spent the whole weekend at Zakkai's house, that he would have followed his regular custom of going to synagogue on Shabbat and that he would have been invited to speak. His invitation to speak is a direct lift from the invitation to Paul in Acts 13.15.

Jesus' talk is made up of the final saying of the Zakkai story, Luke 19.10, followed by the parable of the two sons, recorded in Matthew 21.28-32. This was, I think, inserted by Matthew into Mark's account to make a point, but it seems indisputably a genuine story of Yeshua's. The sermon ends with a quote from Matthew 20.16.

[2]When Jesus used the expression 'son of man' we do not know if he used the Hebrew 'ben-adam', or the Aramaic 'bar-enosh'. Both of them normally meant simply 'a man' or 'I'. The prophecy in Daniel 7.13 uses the Aramaic term. It is a highly contentious part of Biblical scholarship.

[3]'Rested in obedience to the commandment' is taken from Luke 23.56.

[4]A suggestion. Was there a visit late in the evening from a couple of representatives of the Essene community of Qumran? It meant walking for two and a half hours, not an obvious thing to do but possible in the moonlight; the moon was almost full. I think that Jesus and his followers must have had some contact with the Essenes, simply because they are mentioned nowhere in the New Testament, although Josephus tells us how influential they were before 70 AD. Perhaps they were the main Jewish religious group apart from the followers of John the Baptist whom Jesus regarded as allies. And did these men perhaps leave very early the next day to prepare for Jesus' arrival at Jerusalem alongside the Essene community in Jerusalem?

10th Nisan

Four days before Passover

Walking to Jerusalem[1]

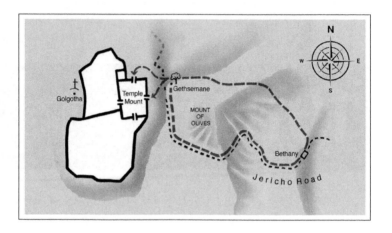

They got up before dawn. Zakkai supplied the group with a high quality breakfast of wheat bread and oil, dates, and wine mixed with water. None of that coarse barley bread they were used to in the Galil! They set out in the early morning sunlight with a spring in their step. They quickly attracted a large crowd of well-wishers, accompanying them through the smart streets of the well-to-do part of Yericho. As they approached the dusty, rocky start of the road as it left the fertile plain, the people of Yericho saw a familiar sight - Bar-Timai[2], the blind beggar. (No one seemed to know his first name). He had sat at the same spot for twenty years, ever since he caught an eye disease from another child).

"Brothers, what's all this crowd? You're not all going up to Yerushalayim, surely?"

"Brother, it's a great day for us. We're seeing off the prophet Yeshua from Natzeret. He stayed with us all weekend - at the house of Zakkai, would you believe!"

The blind beggar shouted out, *"Yeshua, Ben-David, take pity on me!"*

"Bar-Timai, what are you thinking of, using the Hebrew royal title like that. You'll get us all into trouble."

"Yeshua, Ben-David, take pity on me!!"

"That's enough, Bar-Timai, stop your noise, enough already!"

"BEN-DAVID, TAKE PITY ON ME!!!"

Yeshua had walked on several yards since the beggar had started asking about him. He now stopped, and said, *"Tell him to come here."*

"Courage, brother, get up, he's asking for you."

The blind beggar jumped up, tossing aside his cloak, and ran stumbling in the direction of where he thought Yeshua was standing, helped by members of the crowd. Yeshua grasped the man's shoulders, so he was standing upright facing him.

"So - what do you want me to do for you?"

"Rabbani, let me see again!"

Yeshua paused, his hands still on the beggar's shoulders. Then he announced, *"Your trust has already healed you."*

Then Yeshua kissed him on both cheeks.

The man stood stock still. He blinked several times, rubbed his eyes with the back of his hands, then cried out, *"I CAN SEE! PRAISE GOD! Rabbani, can I come with you?"*[3]

Yeshua's face broke into a broad smile. *"Certainly. Come along."* Yeshua spoke to the trainee in charge of the group's money, Y'hudah Bar-Shimon from K'riot, to make sure that the former beggar had what he needed, then he strode smartly up the steep rocky road that led towards the Temple. Bar-Timai ran back to collect his cloak - he would need it in the chilly Yerushalayim night air - and followed Yeshua on the way.

The road was partially paved during the steep ascent from Yericho past Herod's castle. It flattened a bit where it joined Wadi Qelt. Here Yeshua and his followers refilled their leather water bottles, for there would be no more water for the next fourteen miles. The path was sometimes paved and sometimes bare limestone rock. It was hot, dry and dusty work. An hour later they passed the Roman garrison guarding the pass of Adummim, a favourite spot for bandit attacks. They had now walked for almost three hours, uphill all the way. The angle of ascent would be easier for the next six hours, and Yeshua and his followers sat for a rest among the shrubs which gave some relief from the glare of the sun on the rocky surface.

"It's a tough journey. But it'll be worth it when we see Israel saved!" said one of the followers.

"Yes, brother, the day of liberation!" exclaimed his friend.

Yeshua sighed heavily, and the group grew quiet as they waited for him to speak.

"Boys and girls, you're looking forward to a real regime change, yes?"

"Yes." "Amen." "Truly", were the murmured responses.

The group fell silent as Yeshua spoke:

"Let me tell you about one. It happened when I was a baby. When Herod the tyrant died he had already killed three of his sons. The eldest survivor, Archelaus, claimed the throne and went to Caesar in Rome to have it confirmed. Before Archelaus left, he gathered together ten of his senior officials and lent them each ten thousand pounds and told them to trade with it and make a profit while he was away. But the people hated him and sent a delegation to implore Caesar to appoint someone else, especially as he had just killed three thousand protesters in the Temple itself.

"As you know, Archelaus received the kingship of Judaea and Samaria from Caesar. His brothers were made kings over parts of the Galil. When Archelaus returned to Yerushalyim three months

later, he held a public audience. Each of the officials were called forward in turn.

"One said that his trading had been very successful, and he had turned his ten thousand pounds into a hundred thousand pounds. "Excellent," said the king, "You have been reliable in a small matter, I will make you governor over ten cities."

"Another said he had turned his ten into fifty thousand pounds. 'Excellent,' said the king, 'You have been reliable in a small matter, I will make you governor over five cities.'

"Finally, the last one stepped forward and said, 'Lord, when you left I took your money and wrapped it up in a cloth and hid it so it would be safe. Because I know that you are a hard man. You squeeze a profit out of what you haven't invested in, and take from what you haven't contributed anything to. So I was scared, and decided to keep your ten thousand pounds safe. Here it is.'

"His lord said, 'You evil servant! You knew that I was a hard man, squeezing a profit out of what I haven't invested, taking from what I haven't contributed anything to? Instead of hiding the money away, why didn't you at least give it to investment bankers so I would get the interest? But no - you wanted to keep your head below the parapet, didn't you? So - take this unreliable slave's money and give it to the one with the hundred thousand. And think yourself lucky I don't treat you worse.

'As for those enemies of mine who didn't want me to be king, bring them here before me right now. I want to see their heads cut off, right here, right now.' "[4]

"The group sat in stunned silence. After a pause, Yeshua said, 'Right, lads, let's get moving. We need to get to Yerushalyim while it is still day."

From Bethany to Jerusalem (and back)

It was mid-afternoon by the time they climbed the final steep ascent. The road skirted round Beit-Anyah[5] with its imposing two-storey hostel for the destitute. To everyone's surprise, Yeshua stopped walking and sat down, with the Temple on the other side of the Kidron valley actually in sight. He called a couple of his trainees and said,

"See the village the other side of the valley, Beit-Pagey[5], with its groves of fig trees? That's where you need to go. As you enter it, you'll find a colt, a young horse[6], tied up outside a house. It may be a bit skittish, because no one's yet ridden it. Untie it, and bring it here. If anyone challenges you, say, 'The master needs it,' and they'll let you take it."

Everyone enjoyed the opportunity to catch their breath after nine hours' hard walking. Some time later, the two trainees came dragging along a beautiful young horse, chestnut with a white blaze on its forehead. It was clearly not yet broken in. It was skittish, pawing the ground and dancing its back legs from side to side.

Yeshua walked slowly towards the nervous horse. *"Ti ragah habibi, be calm, my darling. We're friends, no?"* He stroked the horse's neck and gradually the colt became still. Yeshua walked to the side of the road and found some long grass by a wall. He took a handful and offered it to the colt. *"Here, my dear. Friends, yes?"* The young horse gave a little whinny and nuzzled up to this kind man. Yeshua spoke to the two men who had brought the colt.

"Keep hold of the rope, so she doesn't take fright at anything. No bridle, no reins. I hereby appoint you horse officers of the kingdom. You're in charge of her until we bring her back safely to Beit-Pagey."

Bar-Timaius ran through the group, saying, *"Rabbi, here, take my cloak. Horses have bony backs!"* One of the group put his hands together to help Yeshua onto the horse. In a moment Yeshua was sitting serenely on his steed. Smiling, he said, *"Forward to Yerushalayim!"*

The whole group, over a hundred men and women, started praising God and crying out, *"HOSANNA! BLESSED IS HE WHO COMES IN ADONAI'S NAME![7] HOSANNA!"* Some cut down branches and waved them. Others put their cloaks on the path in front of Yeshua's horse. The procession made its way over the shoulder of the Mount of Olives. Where the path turned left to descend sharply down the hill, with the Tombs of the Prophets on the left, Yeshua stopped. Everyone also stopped as Yeshua gazed at the city spread out before him, the magnificent towers, the tiled roofs, the ostentatious facade of the Temple silhouetted against the late afternoon sun, and, dominating the whole city, the enormous Roman fortress of the Antonia. Silent tears started to run down Yeshua's cheeks into his beard. Suddenly, he raised his voice, keening a lament:

> "Yerushalayim, Yerushalayim!
> You kill the prophets!
> You stone the ones sent to you!
> How often I've wanted to gather your children,
> as a hen gathers her chicks,
> and you would not.
> If only you'd known today
> what makes for your shalom[8],
> but it's hidden from your eyes.
> The days are coming upon you
> when your enemies will encircle you,
> dash you to the ground,
> you and your children within you,
> and leave not a single stone
> on a stone standing
> all because you did not recognise
> the hour you'll be held to account.[9]

After another moment silently taking in sight of the city, Yeshua set off down the hill, with his followers behind him. On either side of the path were hundreds of booths, temporary shelters put up by pilgrims, but with few people around. Most were still in the Temple. Only a few women and children cheered as the procession wound its way down to the river Kidron. As they reached the bottom, they started meeting pilgrims coming out of the Temple. As soon as they were told that the prophet Yeshua from the Galil was making a grand entrance, excitement swelled rapidly. As more pilgrims joined them, the ones from the Galil shouting particularly loudly and exuberantly.

"PRAISE ELOHA! PRAISE ADONAI THE KING OF ISRAEL!
BLESSED IS HE WHO COMES IN THE NAME OF ADONAI!
BLESSED IS THE COMING KINGDOM OF OUR FATHER DAVID!"

Some of them took off their cloaks and spread them on the path, so that the way leading to the Eastern Gate became a royal carpet.

When they got to the Gate, Yeshua dismounted. Most of the pilgrims turned back to rejoin their families in the pilgrims' camps. Yeshua asked the two 'horse officers' to look after the colt and made sure that Bar-Timai had his cloak back. Two hasidim were leaving the Temple just then and said to Yeshua, *"Rabbi, it's not fitting for such things to be spoken of you, a mere man, and here on the sacred stones of the Temple."* Yeshua smiled at them and said, *"Amen, amen, if these were silent, the stones you speak of would be shouting."*

He then strode past them and the Temple guards into the Temple itself.

It would not be long before the gates were closed for the night. Shadows were already lengthening. Jesus walked around the vast space of the Outer Court like any ordinary tourist, taking in the activity of the merchants who were now closing down their money-changing services; the sheep and cattle dealers, starting to drive their animals back to their pens outside the North Gate; the labourers sweeping up the dung-covered straw from the marble pavement. As he approached the centre of the Temple complex, the Court of Israel in front of the Court of the Priests, the smell of burning flesh, smoke, incense and fresh blood formed a rather sickly smell. Yeshua took it all in, but not one word or expression on his face indicated what he thought. The twelve trainees followed him closely, always ready to leap to his defence should the authorities try to detain him. As the first oil lamps were lit, Yeshua said, "Time to go, boys." He led them outside the city, and together with the colt, made the hour's walk back to Beit-Anyah.

Notes for 10th Nisan/Sunday

[1]Sources are Mark 10.46-52, Luke 19.11-28, and the web article 'From Jerusalem to Jericho' from the American Bible Society. These are followed by Mark 11.1-11 and Luke 19.20-44.

[2]Bar-Timai is the Aramaic equivalent of Bartimaeus. Timaeus is the Greek word meaning value or honour.

[3]'Rabbani' means 'great teacher' - see John 20.16

[4]The chilling story which Yeshua tells is the only one of his stories which is based on a historical event. Matthew has a different version of it in 25.14-30, but he abstracts it from the historical situation.

[5]Beit Anyah was the Aramaic name for Bethany and meant House of Affliction. I have guessed that there was a hostel there for impoverished people.

Beit-Pagey we know as Bethphage, and means House of Unripe Figs.

[6]The word translated colt was normally used for a young horse, though it could be the young of other animals. The idea that it was an ass or a donkey comes simply from Matthew's and John's use of the prophecy of Zechariah 9.9, the Septuagint Greek translation. If you take Mark at face value, as I do, then it was a young horse. Shame, really, because G K Chesterton wrote a fine poem called "The Donkey".

[7]'Adonai' is Hebrew for 'Lord'. It was used in place of saying the sacred name of God YHWH.

[8]Shalom' means peace, but much more than just peace. It implies health, wealth, prosperity and being within God's circle of blessing.

[9]A conflation of Luke 13.34 and 19.41-44, edited.

11th Nisan

Three days before Passover[1]

Bethany - a feast[2,3]

Bethany or Al-Eizariya c.1900

A mixed group of men and women trudged uphill to Beit-Anyah. They separated at the entrance of the village, the men trainees, with Shim'on Kepha in the lead, accompanying Yeshua to the mansion of another Shim'on who had only recently come out of quarantine from his disfiguring disease. The women, including Yeshua's mother Miryam, went to stay with El'azar[4] and his two sisters.

The young Miryam met them at the gate with delight.

"It's so wonderful to see you all. You must be so tired. We've got nothing ready for you, because we're all going across to Shim'on's house for a feast. He has a big guest room where we can catch up on all the news. The men, poor dears, will be outside in the courtyard![5]"

Eleazar smiled his welcome. Marta took charge and said, *"Don't mind her, she's so excited to see you all. And Yeshua of course. But come and sit down and we'll have your feet washed. You'll feel properly better after."*

Shim'on's house was built around a large courtyard with the main gate opening on the street. Shim'on met Yeshua and the twelve and kissed each on both cheeks, beard to beard. After two servants had washed the feet of the guests, they put their packs down in the large room where the women were going to eat, then went to stand round the brazier burning in the courtyard. Eleazar entered along with his sisters, and the men settled down to recline around the three sides of the tables. Shim'on asked Yeshua to give the blessing.

He took a small loaf, broke it in half and said,

"Baruch Atah Adonai Eloheynu Melech ha'olam, ha'motzi lechem min ha'aretz. - Blessed are you, Lord our God, King of the universe, who provides bread from the land." He went on to invoke the blessing over the wine. The servants came in and out, refilling the plates of lentils, vegetables and baked fish, supervised by Marta who could not bear for things not to be done properly. Suddenly, the conversation died down. Young Miryam was standing in the doorway of the guest chamber, tears tricking down her cheeks. She entered hesitantly and knelt where Yeshua was reclining.

"Rabbi," she whispered, *"it's thanks to you that our brother is alive."* She started to weep again, choking on her tears. The tears started dripping onto Yeshua's outstretched feet.[6] She took a deep breath, reached up, unpinned her hair and used her long dark hair to wipe away the drops. The trainees and Eleazar shifted uncomfortably on their cushions. Yeshua acted as if nothing out of the ordinary was happening. Miryam reached into a small embroidered cloth bag tied to her belt. From it she took a delicate white translucent alabaster jar, sealed with wax. With a small knife she prised off the wax seal and poured the most wonderful scented oil of nard[7] onto Yeshua's feet, smoothing it gently into the skin with her hands. She bowed down and planted a single kiss on his foot. Then rapidly she got up and went back towards the guest room. Until a man's comment froze her in her tracks.

"Rabbi, that's not right! That's a waste! You tell us always to remember the poor. That nard could have fed thirty people for a month!"

"Let her be, Y'hudah. Why do you trouble her? She's done a beautiful thing for me. You'll always have the poor with you, and you can do good for them whenever you wish. But you won't always have

me. She has done what she could. She has given me my burial anointing in advance."

A shocked murmur ran round the table. Shim'on Kepha hesitantly said, "Rabbi, I don't think we understand."

"No, Shim'on? But you will. Indeed wherever you proclaim the message of Elaha's kingly rule[8] in the whole world, you will tell the story of her gift in memory of her."

Miryam stood transfixed in the doorway as she and her rabbi gazed at each other. Then, with her knees shaking she turned and stumbled back into the guest room where she collapsed in tears.

Notes for 11th Nisan/Sunday evening

[1] The Jewish day started at sunset. The Roman day, and our day, starts theoretically at midnight, though for practical purposes, like parties, the new day starts at dawn. So the two systems frequently are not in sync, as here.

[2] Sources are Mark 14.3-9 and John 12.1-8

[3] In Mark's gospel, the feast at which young Miryam anoints Yeshua's feet is two days before Passover. In John's gospel it is six days before Passover and just before the solemn entry into Jerusalem at the start of the next day. However, I think that Mark's detail that Yeshua arrived late on Palm Sunday is decisive. And it does make sense that the feast is given as a welcome to Yeshua on his arrival, so I have placed it here, three days before Passover. Three days, not four, because the Jewish day started at sunset. On the other hand, if John's timing is correct, then Jesus entered Jerusalem on Palm Thursday.

[4] Eleazar was the Hebrew name of the man we know of as Lazarus, whom Jesus raised from death. Miryam is the Hebrew version of Mary, and every second Jewish woman was called it. It can be confusing!

[5] The domestic arrangements for Yeshua and his followers are my supposition. I don't think that any ordinary large house could accommodate such a large group of both men and women.

[6]Did Miryam pour the ointment over Yeshua's head (as in Mark) or over his feet (as in John). I have chosen the latter simply because, if they were formally reclining at table, it would have been awkward for her to reach his head.

[7]Nard was a thick oil distilled from spikenard, part of the Valerian family, an intense and valuable perfume.

[8]Instead of 'the kingdom of God' I have used 'Elaha's kingly rule'. 'Elaha' is the ordinary Aramaic word for God, 'Kingly rule' denotes the fact that when Jesus talks about the Kingdom of God, he is talking about activity, not territory.

Roman alabaster jar

11th Nisan

Three days before Passover[1]

The Temple - Occupation

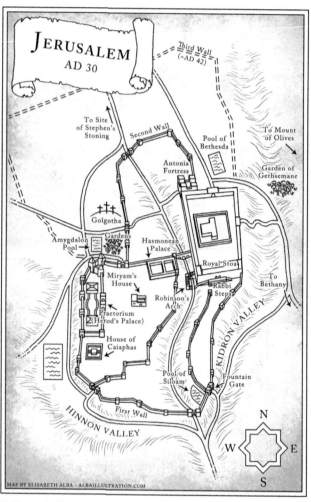

© Elisabeth Alba

The Fig Tree at Bethphage

As the group broke their night-time fast, standing together in the courtyard, Yeshua asked Shim'on if he could give him some lengths of thin rope.

"Of course, Rabbi. But why?"

"Oh Shim'on, you'll certainly hear later" was the playful but serious response.

Yeshua's followers, men and women, gathered in the street and set off through the tens of thousands[2] of home-made booths which the pilgrims had put up for their shelter during the sacred fortnight. Some of the Galileans recognised Yeshua and said, *"Shalom, Rabbi." "Shalom, my friend,"* he replied.

In a few minutes they had reached the neighbouring village of Beit-Pagey'. As they left the village behind them, Yeshua mused, *"Hmmm. Beit-Pagey' - 'House of Unripe Figs'. I wonder if it's true. Maybe we should test it out. I could do with some figs to finish off breakfast."*

He made for a large old fig tree standing untidily on its own on the edge of the hill. He started pushing aside the large leaves, squeezing the hard unripe buds.

"What's he doing?" muttered T'oma to Ya'akov Bar-Chalfai. *"He must know we won't get any figs for a couple of months."*

"Search me," responded Ya'akov.

Yeshua stood back from the tree with an almost comical look of anger on his face. He stretched out his arm, pointing directly at the fig tree and proclaimed, *"You useless fig tree! All leaves and no fruit! In the name of Adonai the King of the universe, you are cursed to be fruitless from now and for ever."* He strode off downhill, calling over his shoulder, *"Come on, lads, let's leave this house of unripe figs behind us."*

All the trainees followed, completely bewildered (not for the first time). Ya'akov Bar-Zavdai said to his brother Yochanan, *"What was all that about? "Not sure,"* his brother replied, *"but did you notice that directly behind the fig tree, as the Rabbi pointed at it, on the other side of the valley, there was the Temple? Maybe it wasn't the fig tree he was cursing, what d'you think?"*

The Temple - Occupation!

At the river Kidron, before the final ascent to the Temple, Yeshua gathered his group around.

"Now, lads and ladies, I must warn you that we are about to have some exciting times. You women, I want you to stay outside until noon, the situation could get violent. Our Father is supposed to be Lord of the Temple. Today he will be. You men, I want you to take control of the gates. I need four on each one - the Eastern Gate, North Gate, Palace Gate and Huldah Gates. Have I got some volunteers? Good. Sort it out among yourselves. My twelve, you stay with me. We're going to get rid of all the money-making, all the trading, all the commercial gain that defiles this holy place."

Yeshua strode up the path to the double arched Eastern Gate, past the Temple guards on duty there and out into the Outer Court, followed closely by his twelve trainees. He went up to one of the largest tables on which the currency exchangers bought Roman money and sold ritually pure Temple coinage. The dealer looked up with a slightly shark-like smile at this imposing but clearly unsophisticated new customer.

"Shalom, my friend, how much money do you want to change? You won't get a better rate than mine in the whole of Yerushalayim."

The tall, bearded northerner with piercing eyes just said, *"Get out."*

"Pardon?"

"Out. Out. Out!" With a rapid two-handed lift he tipped the heavy table up, spilling all the silver coins over the Temple floor. He strode over to the next table. *"OUT!"* he shouted, and tipped that table over too. Soon there was massive confusion with the currency exchangers and the crowd, scrabbling for coins on the marble pavement and other pilgrims joining in the fun.

The Temple guards rushed to the disturbance but were helpless before the manic uproar which now had infected hundreds of the pilgrims. Yeshua took the six pieces of thin rope from his belt and laid about with them right and left, striking cattle, lambs and their owners so that entire Outer Court was filled with shouting and screaming, cattle roaring, sheep baaing, fluttering doves set free from their overturned cages. Too late , the Temple guards realised that they had left all the gateways unattended and that they were now in the hands of burly Galilean pilgrims, looking threateningly pious, and outnumbering the guards two to one.

At each of the gates a traffic jam was developing as traders tried to bring their carts through the Temple as a short cut, only to be met by half a dozen muscled northerners who said, *"You're not going to bring that through here, are you, sunshine?"* And then they couldn't turn round because the cart behind them was blocking their way. It was absolute chaos.

Some Yerushalayim citizens went up to Yeshua, really angry[3].

"What are you playing at? You've got no right to act like this, disrupting our Temple. You'd better show us some sign that you've got God on your side - like turning a stick into a snake or water into blood.[4] Go on, we're waiting."

Yeshua didn't give any ground. He looked intently at the angry group and said, *"You want a sign? All right, here's one. Destroy this temple, and I will raise it up again in three days."*

"You're mad! A lunatic - or worse. It's taken forty six years to build this magnificent Temple. You're going to knock it down and rebuild it in three days! You're having a laugh. But you won't last. That's a promise."

The Roman tribune, looking out at the scene from the Antonia Fortress overlooking the Temple, could see the anarchy, but saw no immediate threat to life. He decided that to intervene would only make matters much much worse. And the Temple authorities were completely wrong-footed. When reports came in that the Galilean preacher Yeshua was responsible, they realised they had to move carefully. *"We'll let him have his day, and tomorrow we'll clip his wings,"* they decided.

The disturbance gradually calmed down, only because the traders and currency exchangers admitted defeat and retreated. The currency exchangers set up their stalls south of the Temple, between the Huldah Gates and the horse-racing stadium. The dealers in animals for sacrifice tied their animals up in groups between the North Gate of the Temple and the Pool of Bethesda.

The Temple - Teaching[5]

Yeshua stood in the middle of Solomon's Portico and proclaimed: *"Brothers and fathers! You know how Elaha has spoken in the Haftorah, 'My house shall be called a house of prayer for all the*

Goyim!' The Torah tells us that we are to be a blessing for all the families on earth! But we have allowed the priests to turn this sacred place into a robbers' cave, a den of thieves! And this at Pesach! My brothers and fathers, let us worship the Holy One, blessed be he, not in mere words, but in spirit and in truth!"

Shouts of approval rose from the crowd which now numbered in thousands. A young man shouldered his way to the front of the crowd.

"Rabbi, Rabbi!" he cried.

"Yes, my son?"

"Rabbi, I appeal to you! My father has just died, and my brother, my elder brother, claims the whole of the inheritance, leaving me with nothing! Tell him to share the inheritance justly, Rabbi, please!"

Yeshua paused as he gazed at the face of the young man, and then scanned the faces of the crowd. He spoke directly to the petitioner.

"Man, who made me a judge or arbitrator over you? That's not what I've come for." Then he cried out to the crowd. "Beware! Beware of greed! All kinds of greed! What you own doesn't define who you are. Let me tell you a story.

"It's about a rich farmer. And you know what farmers are like, always complaining, always looking on the gloomy side of life. Like one farmer who had had an amazing harvest. When he'd stored it all away, he moaned to his neighbours, 'It'll be the most disastrous harvest I've known if this lot catches fire.

"Anyway, this farmer's harvest was so good, he couldn't complain about anything. Except that he hadn't got enough storage space. It was a real puzzle, because, like all farmers, he hated spending money. But this time he reckoned he had no alternative. He had to demolish his existing barns and build several bigger ones. 'Yup,' he said to himself, 'Once these are built, I'll really have it made. It'll be several years before I have to worry about another harvest. I can sit back and enjoy life. Oh yes, and I'll need a decent wine store.'

"But guess what? That very night God spoke to him. Know what he said? 'You fool!' That's what he said. 'You fool. This is your last night on earth. By the morning you'll be dead. Then who's going to enjoy your new big barns?'

"That is what everyone is like who wants to be rich in money but isn't rich towards Elaha."

At the end of the afternoon, Yeshua led the twelve out of the Temple and back to the bridge over the Kidron. On the other side Yeshua stopped and said, "Listen, lads, we're not going to stick together all the time. If we get separated, we'll meet at dusk at this olive orchard."

"But Rabbi, there are lots of olive orchards here. What's the name of this one?"

Y'hudah Bar-Shim'on from K'riot spoke. "I know it, Rabbi. It's called after the oil press in the middle, Gat Sh'manim."[6]

Notes for 11th Nisan/Monday

[1]Sources: Mark 12.1-19, Luke 12.13-21, John 2.18-22

[2]According to the Jewish historian Josephus writing about 80 AD, there were about 2,700,000 pilgrims around Jerusalem at Passover. The festival lasted from a week before Passover to the end of the week after it.

[3]The exchange between the group of Jerusalemites taken from John 2.18-22 is certainly historical, because it formed the main charge against Jesus at his trial. In John the confrontation is sparked off by 'Jews'.

This could refer to the Jewish authorities, or to people from Judaea (as opposed to Galilee). I have chosen the latter.

[4]The stick into snake and water into blood are the two signs that Moses did in front of Pharaoh to back up his demand that the Hebrew slaves should be allowed to leave Egypt. (Exodus 7.8-24)

[5]We are told that after the removal of the traders, the crowd were captivated by Yeshua's teaching (Mark 12.18). But we have no record of what he taught. I have use a teaching incident from earlier in Yeshua's ministry in Luke 12.13-21 to fill in the gap.

[6]'Gat Sh'manim' is 'Gethsemane'.

12th Nisan

Two days before Passover

The Temple - Confrontation[1]

Model of the temple, Israel Museum
Berthold Werner, public domain

The Fig Tree Again

Yeshua and his followers set out early the next day. After passing through Beit-Pagey', they all noticed the leafless skeleton of a fig tree.

"Look, Rabbi," said Shim'on Kefa, *"that fig tree you cursed yesterday - it's dead! Withered from the ground up! How could that happen?"*

Yeshua stopped and contemplated the dead tree, its bare branches pointing like prayer hands into the early morning sky. He looked over his shoulder at his trainees. *"Keep your focus on the Father. Then whatever you say will happen. In fact if you say to that mountain over there,"* he nodded towards the Temple dominating the Kidron valley, *"Be uprooted and thrown into the sea, it will happen."* He smiled at his trainees' dumbfounded expressions, and said, *"Come on, lads, let's go"*.

Confrontation with the Temple authorities

They arrived at the Temple just as the morning service of psalm-singing and sacrifice was ending. Already each gate was manned by four temple guards and an equal number of Galilean pilgrims, looking at each other warily, but beginning to talk to each other. *"So, this prophet of yours, what does he actually say?" "He's challenging, mate, but it's not just his talks, it's the healings he does..."*

Yeshua led his group through both parts of the Outer Court, replying courteously to a number of questioners. The Court was calm, a few groups of both men and women talking together. Many were standing by themselves, swaying devoutly while intoning their prayers. A gentle murmur enveloped the sunlit space. As Yeshua strolled towards the line of pillars that made up Solomon's Portico on the east wall, there was an excited hubbub behind him. He turned to see a small crowd coalescing round a group of a dozen leading priests, Torah-teachers and official members of the Great Council. The crowd swelled with many eager to see the coming confrontation between the Jerusalem authorities and the prophet from the Galil.

Yeshua stood on the platform, which gave him a six inch advantage, and turned round. The leading priests in their spotless white tunics and turbans and scarlet sashes, with the half dozen Torah-teachers and judges in their long brown and black cloaks, looked decidedly impressive. One of the leading priests spoke.

"We are the priests of this holy house, appointed in direct succession from Aaron, the first chief priest of our nation. Also here are Torah-teachers who have studied for years in highly reputable academies. And some of the members of the Great Council who have ultimate authority for the laws and religion of all Israel. Kindly tell us where you have studied, who gave you the rank of teacher, what is your authority for dictating what should or should not take place in this house dedicated to the Holy One, blessed be he."

Yeshua stood completely relaxed as he looked in turn at each member of the impressive delegation in front of him. He noted the different attitudes in the crowd, some murmuring, *"Rabbi, stand up to them!"* Others muttering, *"Here's where this parvenu gets his comeuppance."*

Yeshua took a deep breath, smiled slightly and said, *"That's a fair question. It deserves an answer. I will give you an answer. Providing you answer a question I will ask. You all know Yochanan, who practised his ministry of baptism not twenty miles from here." A buzz of recognition rose from the crowd. "Well now, Yochanan's ministry, was it a call from Adonai Eloheynu, or was it his own idea, a human invention? Tell us."*

The leading priests and Torah-teachers hesitated, looking at each other. *"We need to consult"*, said a leading priest, and the delegation withdrew to a quiet corner of the Outer Court.

"We can't say his call was from God. He was a mountebank[2]. Even called us a brood of vipers."

"We're not popular with anyone. We even fight among ourselves. Maybe it's time for us to give some recognition to their Yochanan. He was devout, though rather extreme. And above all, he's dead, and it would put the Galilean on the spot."

"That's possible, but only if we forget his main platform, which was baptising Jews. We all know what baptism is for. It's not a ritual washing like the obsessive practice of the Essenes. It's going under the water, giving up your life. It's what we expect the Goyim, the Gentiles[3], to do if they want to join the community of Yisrael - as well as having their foreskin circumcised of course. And that's right, because they have to give up their old life and make a brand new start. But this Yochanan called his fellow Jews to be baptised! As if there was no difference between Yisrael and the Goyim. As if in fact we Israelites are Gentiles! He basically excommunicated everyone who disagreed with him. Including us!"

"We have to be careful. This ignorant crowd know nothing of the Torah, they all believe that Yochanan was a great prophet. This Yeshua has already used the crowd to kick the perfectly legal traders out of the Temple. He could turn them against us in a flash. It's just too dangerous."

"We'll just have to put the best face we can on it."

The group of leading priests, Torah-teachers and Council members walked back to Yeshua with as much dignity as they could muster.

"Well, gentlemen, what is your answer?"

"We have considered carefully, and have decided that there are so many issues at stake, that we can't make a definitive statement at this moment."

"Then neither will I tell you what my authority is for standing up for the holiness of this place."

A Pointed Story

Yeshua's gaze shifted to include the whole of the crowd that had gathered.

"I have a story to tell you."

Instantly the crowd became quiet and attentive. The priests and Council members were stuck there in front of Yeshua, unless they wanted to leave looking like undignified losers.

"There was a once a rich man, living in Cyprus, who bought up an estate in the land of Y'hudah."[4]

A hiss of anger rose from the crowd.

"This man sent his steward over to organise the construction of a vineyard during the winter months. He hired local farmers at the minimum wage to clear the ground, build a wall to keep out pests, plant thorn bushes on the outside that would be fully grown after a couple of years, put up a stone watch-tower, chiselled out a two-chamber wine-press, dug holes for sturdy posts at ten-foot intervals, strung cords tight to make a trellis and finally planted the seeds. Back-breaking work! Then the steward hired four of these

local farmers to keep an eye on the vineyard and make sure that some wine did get produced in three years' time.

"The tenants didn't have much to do at first, so they did the only sensible thing. In the rows between the vine saplings they planted a load of onions, leeks and cucumbers. Over the summer, they made a tidy profit. Then in the autumn, who should turn up but a man who said he'd come from the owner in Cyprus, wanting a cut from the profit they had made from the vegetables they had grown. Well, you can guess, they sent him away with a flea in his ear!"

The crowd chuckled at the farmers' chutzpah.

"The absentee landowner didn't blame his servant. He just said, "Maybe they didn't realise you went on my say-so. We'll try again next year."

"Next year, just after Sukkot, another servant came and showed a letter from the landowner. He asked for a fifth of the profit from the vegetables the farmers had harvested. The tenant-farmers got angry. 'Here we are, doing all the work, and this rich guy sits in his villa and expects a cut, when the vines aren't even producing any decent fruit!' Other villagers began to gather round the arguing men and at last rich man's servant decided that discretion was the better part of valour, and he also retreated back to Cyprus.

"The next autumn, the owner's son said, 'Listen father, let me go. Maybe they didn't think that servants you sent there the last two years had the authority to act on your behalf. But they will recognise me, and now that there will be some grapes, there is no reason for them to refuse to give us some return on our investment.' 'Perhaps you're right,' the father said, 'Go, but be careful.'

"The son arrived at the village. It was clear who he was, not only because of the expensive clothes he wore, but also his father's signet ring which the farmers recognised. He began negotiations. There was some argument over how much of the grapes were the *landowner's property. The farmers suggested they harvest some of the grapes and sell them because the grapes were not yet ready for wine-making, and then they would hand the money over to the landowner's son.*

"But that night, the tenant-farmers got together. 'Why did this guy come instead of another servant? Do you think the old man's died? After all, he's got his signet ring. And if the old man is dead, this guy is the heir! If something happened to him, the vineyard would have no owner, and it'd be first come, first served. We'd be sitting pretty!'

"Next day, when the son came to conclude negotiations, one of the farmers brought a large rock crashing down on the back of his head, and the others joined in, beating him to death. They took his body and threw it on the side of the road outside the vineyard, as if he had been killed by brigands. But that deceived nobody."

The crowd shifted uncomfortably. The story had not ended in a way they had expected.

"So - what do you think the rich man in Cyprus will do when he hears about it?"

"He'll be mad with fury" said someone in the crowd. *"He'll get soldiers and kill those farmers. And then he'll let out the vineyard to some honest men."*

"I think so," said Yeshua. He looked directly at the delegation in front of him. *"The vineyard-keepers will be replaced."*

The group of leading priests, Torah-teachers and Council members were dumbfounded at the implied attack. Yeshua spoke again.

"Perhaps you have never read or understood what is written in the Readings[5]. What we sing every year in the Pesach Hallel:[6]
> *"The stone that the builders rejected*
> *has become the chief cornerstone."*

Yeshua stood, dominating the crowd by his presence, silently challenging the authorities to respond. A Council member whispered to one of the leading priests, *"Why don't you get the Temple guards to arrest him?"* The priest whispered back. *"Not the right time. Don't worry, his time will come."*

They made their way back out of the crowd with as much dignity as they could muster, while one brave bystander intoned a poem from the prophet Yesha'yahu:

> *For the vineyard of the Lord of hosts*
> > *is the house of Israel,*
> *and the people of Judah*
> > *are his pleasant planting;*
> *he expected justice, (mishpat)*
> > *but saw bloodshed; (mispah)*
> *righteousness, (tzedakhah)*
> > *but heard a cry! (tze'akhah)[7]*

As they left, Yeshua spoke out:

"Beware of the Torah-teachers, who like to walk around in long robes, and to be greeted with respect in the market places, and to have the best seats in the assembly halls and places of honour at feasts! They swallow down widows' houses and for the sake of appearance say long prayers. They will suffer the greater punishment!"[8]

Enemies gather

As the Temple delegation moved away, a small group of Hasidim[9] and Liberal Jews[9] approached them.

"My lords," said a Hasid, *"Can we have a word?"*

One of the priests said irritably, *"Well, what is it? I doubt if you've come to defend the honour of this holy place."*

"My lord, that is just why we've come. Perhaps a word in private?"

"Follow us to the Hall of Polished Stone[10] - the Council Chamber. We won't be interrupted there."

Once inside the magnificent Hall of Polished Stone, the leading priest sat down, while the rest stood before him.

"Well, you're an unusual group. I am surprised you agree about anything."[11]

A Hasid became the spokesman of the group.

"My lords, it is true that those of us who are devout and devoted to the Torah, we often disagree with our friends here who support our ruler Herod's policy of appeasement, appeasing both those who want to stay faithful to the Torah and those who want to live alongside the Goyim with their looser standards. However, for both of us the Galil Goyim is a peaceful place. We know where the boundaries are, we know not to overstep them. But this Yeshua delights in blurring these boundaries, so that people don't know where they stand. For instance, he goes out of his way to heal people on the Shabbat, often in the middle of our Shabbat prayers. Now he is bringing the same disruption to this house of God."

The seated priest smiled grimly.

"You haven't had much success in reining him in in your Galil, have you?"

"Sadly, no. The mob think he's the manna from heaven. But we and our friends from Herod's side think we have found a way to prick his bubble popularity. Just one misstep on his part, and we think your troubles, and our troubles, will be over."

The Evening Sacrifice[12]

An air of expectancy settled over the Temple as the hour of the afternoon sacrifice approached. Some moved into the Court of Yisrael, also called the Court of Women, because women were allowed to stand round the sides. Others, including Yeshua and his trainees, remained in the Outer Court, but stood facing the Holy Place. Trumpets sounded as the heavy interior gates were opened. The lamb was killed and prepared for the sacrificial offering, made on behalf of all Yisrael. The menorah oil lamps were cleaned and relit. A deep silence enveloped the whole of the Temple. In the stillness one could hear the Shema[13] intoned: *"Shema, Israel, Adonai Eloheynu, Adonai echad..."*.

Those inside the Court of Israel could hear the thanksgiving prayer: *"We praise you, Adonai Eloheynu, God of our fathers, God of all flesh, our Creator and the Creator from the beginning! Blessing and praise be to your great and holy name, that you have preserved us in life and kept us. So preserve and keep us, and gather the dispersed ones into your holy courts, to keep your laws, and to do your good pleasure, and to serve you with our whole heart, as we dedicate ourselves to you this day. Baruch atah Adonai, to whom belongs praise."*

In the silence, men and women stood with their eyes closed, their hands uplifted in adoration, whispering their own prayers. Some of Yeshua's trainees whispered the prayer he had taught them:

"Abba - may your name be truly praised - may your kingly rule come - give us our needful bread - forgive us our debts, as we forgive those indebted to us - protect us from the time of testing."[14]

The smell of roast meat wafted through the courts as the pieces of the lamb were offered on the altar, together with the high priest's offering of twelve half loaves and the wine of the drink-offering which was thrown against the side of the altar. The silver trumpets sounded as the incense offering was burned. The choir of assistant priests sang the psalm of the day, accompanied by harps and flutes:

> *"God has taken his place in the divine council;*
> *in the midst of the gods he holds judgement."*[15]

Three calls from the silver trumpets signalled the end of the service. Everyone began making their way slowly past the massive gates and out to the workaday world. Yeshua and his trainees walked down to the Kidron and back up the Mount of Olives to Beit-Anyah.

Notes to 12th Nisan/Tuesday

[1] Sources are Mark 11.20 - 12.12; 12.38-40.

[2] A mountebank is a person who sells quack medicines, as from a platform in public places, attracting and influencing an audience by tricks, storytelling, etc

[3] St Paul lists the advantages of the Jews: "They are Israelites, and to them belong the adoption (as God's children), the glory, the covenants, the giving of the law, the worship, and the promises; to them belong the patriarchs, and from them, according to the flesh, comes the Messiah." (Romans 9.4-5) The Gentiles were scorned because of idolatrous worship of many different gods. Jews were unique in the ancient world in not having any images of God.

[4] The story of the vineyard tenants occurs in four gospels, Matthew, Mark, Luke and the Coptic Gospel of Thomas. All are slightly different. Thomas' account could well be the earliest. The passages are Mark 12.I-12, Luke 20.9-19, Matthew 21.33-46, Thomas 65, 66. Following J Jeremias, 'The Parables of Jesus', I assume that the owner is an absentee landlord, possible Gentile, and therefore the classic 'bad guy' to Yeshua's audience.

[5] Yeshua uses the term 'Readings' or 'Mikra' rather than the mediaeval Jewish term 'Tenakh' to refer to all the Hebrew Scriptures. 'Readings' refer to everything that was read publicly. Jesus regularly used the

phrase 'the Law and the Prophets', the Torah and the Haftorah, but that did not include the Psalms, so he could have used the wider term 'Readings'.

[6]The quote about the cornerstone comes from Psalm 118.22. It is part of the Hallel, meaning Praise, the group of Psalms 113 - 118 which was sung at the end of every Passover meal.

[7]The quote about the vineyard is from Isaiah 5.7, a familiar passage to Jews.

[8]I have moved this attack on the scribes/Torah-teachers from the end of chapter 12 to this point as it makes dramatic sense.

[9]The word 'Pharisee' has had such a bad press in the Christian world, that I find it is better to use instead the term 'Hasidim'. This has been used since the 17th century for ultra-devout Jews, as well as for a 2nd centre BCE group which eventually amalgamated with the Pharisees (in Hebrew P'rushim).

Herodians were presumably more liberal Jews who accepted Herod Antipas' rapprochement between Jewish faith and Greek civilisation. They disappeared after the Jewish war of 66 - 73, and only re-appeared in the Liberal and Reform movements in 19th century Germany.

[10]The Hall of Polished Stone was the large room to the side of the Court of Israel which was set apart for meetings of the Temple authorities, particularly full meetings of the Sanhedrin or Great Council. Also known as the Court of Uncut Stone, or Court of Hewn Stone.

[11]The conversations between the priests and the Hasidim from Galilee is pure invention. However, it is curious that the challenge to Yeshua in Mark 12.13-17 comes from a mixed group of Pharisees and Herodians. Apart from here, we only read about them in the story of the healing of the man with the withered hand in a Galilean synagogue (Mark 3.1-6). Here I assume that these men came to the Passover Festival along with everyone else, and, while there, seized the opportunity to take their radical rabbi down a peg or two. Alternatively, it could have been a debate that took place in Galilee and was transposed by Mark to Jesus' final week.

[12]The description of the worship in the Temple is taken from 'The Temple - its Ministry and Services as they were in the time of Jesus Christ' by Alfred Edersheim (1874)

[13]'Shema!' means 'Hear!', and refers to Deuteronomy 6.4, "Hear, O Israel, the LORD your God, the LORD is one..." Since at least the 2nd century, BCE Jews have used the word 'Adonai' or Lord, instead of the sacred name of God, YHWH, which stopped being pronounced, so we only have the consonants, not the vowels.

[14]The Lord's Prayer is taken from Luke's vision in Luke 11.2-4. The petition "Give us this day our daily bread" is probably wrong, because no one knows what the Greek word translated 'daily' means. It is used nowhere else. It could mean 'tomorrow's' or 'necessary'.

[15]The Psalm for the evening sacrifice on Tuesday was Psalm 82 (Edersheim).

13th Nisan

One day before Passover

The Temple - Disputes[1]

Solomon's Portico

Dispute with Hasidim

Yeshua and his trainees got to the Temple during the prayers
after the morning sacrifice. After the blessing, he made his way to
Solomon's Portico[2] and started talking to the crowd that instantly
gathered in front of him. A small group of Galilean Hasidim and
Liberal supporters of Herod made their way to the front, the crowd
parting respectfully.

"Shalom, Rabbi," they said.

"Shalom aleikhem."

*"Rabbi, you have a great reputation at home in the Galil. We know
you speak the truth without fear or favour. Now, we have a question,
which we would like you to answer in this holy place. It is at the
heart of how we can be the chosen people in this day and age.
So please give us your judgement. The taxes which the Roman
emperor, Caesar, demands of us, is it right for us to pay or not?"*

The crowd began to dispute excitedly. *"Of course it's wrong, we
are the free people of the Lord!"* *"We've got no choice, they've got
their soldiers here, even looking down on us right now from the
Antonia".* *"How can we bear being in subjection to the Goyim?"* *"But
we're free to worship, and they allow us raise taxes from Jews in
the Dispersion to support the Temple."* *"You can't make money more
important than freedom!"*

Yeshua regarded the group of Hasidim and Liberals, as well as the excited crowd with an ironic eye.

"My friends, you have asked a hard question. You'll have to help me a bit. Have any of you got a denarius on you?"

"Yes, rabbi," said one, handing it up.

Yeshua took it and examined it carefully. The crowd grew silent in anticipation.

"Tebu lak[3]" he said, handing it back. *"Tell me, what does the inscription say?"*

"Caesar Augustus."

"And whose image is on the coin?"

"Caesar Augustus."

"Then give to Caesar what belongs to Caesar, and to Elaha what belongs to Elaha."

The Hasidic delegation stood with their mouths open while the crowd burst into ecstatic applause. Muttering to each other, the Hasidim and Herod's supporters extricated themselves from the crowd and went back to the Hall of Polished Stone to report their failure to the Temple authorities.

Dispute with the Temple aristocrats[4]

Some time later there was a stir in the crowd as an impressive group of Temple aristocrats made their away towards Yeshua, their lavishly embroidered coats and turbans making a striking contrast with the simple brown cloak worn by Yeshua. The crowd settled into a resentful silence.

"Rabbi, we have a case which we would like your opinion on," said the leading Temple aristocrat.

"Go on," said Yeshua.

"In the Torah, Moshe laid down this rule:

'When brothers reside together, and one of them dies and has no son, the wife of the deceased shall not be married outside the family to a stranger. Her husband's brother shall go in to her, taking her in marriage, and performing the duty of a husband's brother to her, and the firstborn whom she bears shall succeed to the name of the deceased brother, so that his name may not be blotted out of Israel."[5]

"Now just this happened among us. There were seven brothers, and the eldest married a woman, but he died before she could conceive."

"Then the second brother married the woman, and he died before she conceived. The third brother married her, but he died too before anything happened."

"Sounds like Tobiah's Sarah[6] to me," shouted a man in the crowd.

The Temple aristocrat smiled condescendingly.

"Quite so. The fourth brother's funeral was just a few days after the wedding. The fifth brother lasted longer but again the woman had no children to carry on the family name. The sixth brother fared no better. And the seventh, the lucky seventh, also perished without any children. In the end, the woman herself died."

"About time too!" "Worn out, was she?" A guffaw of laughter came from the back of the crowd.

"Now, Rabbi, your judgement please. In the so-called resurrection, which you and the Hasidim believe in so devoutly, whose wife will she be? All seven of the brothers had had her."

A buzz of hilarity and curiosity issued from the crowd.

Yeshua's face showed not a hint of humour.

"Isn't this why you aristocrats go so wrong? You think you revere the Torah, but you haven't even begun to understand it. You have no clue about either the Readings or the power of Elaha. When men and women rise from the dead, they neither marry nor are given in marriage. They are like the messengers whom Elaha sends out[7], spiritual beings in the life beyond. And as for the dead being raised, haven't you even read the Torah[8] itself? How in the passage about the burning bush, Elaha said to Moshe, 'I am Elohim of Avraham, and Elohim of Yitzchak, and Elohim of Ya'akov.'[8] He is not Elohim of the dead but of the living. You are quite wrong."

The crowd burst into applause. The Temple aristocrats grimaced, then angrily shouldered their way out of the crowd. One muttered, "You see? Just another of these new-fangled rabble-rousers. No learning. No respect for tradition."

Yeshua took a deep breath and perceptibly relaxed. "Well, my friends, let me ask you a question. Ha-Mashiach[9], who is his father? Whose son is he?"

A few voices called out, "Son of David!"

"Indeed, that is what the Torah-teachers tell us. But then, how come that David himself, inspired by Ruach Ha-Kodesh[10], says in the Readings,

> Adonai says to my Adonai,
> 'Sit at my right hand
> until I make your enemies your footstool.'

David himself calls him Lord - Adonai. So how can he be David's son?"

Another outburst of clapping at this crafty bit of Bible exegesis.

A Torah-teacher's Question[11]

A Torah-teacher in the crowd, easily identified by his long-sleeved tunic and black cloak, pushed his way forward.

"Rabbi, I have heard your discussion with our friends the Temple aristocrats. May I be permitted to put a question to you?"

"Surely"

"What then is the first commandment in all the Torah? How do you read it?"

Yeshua stood up straight with his arms outstretched and recited, *"The first commandment is, 'Shema, Yisrael, Adonai Eloheynu, Adonai echad,[12] and you shall love Adonai Eloheynu with all your heart and with all your soul and with all your mind, and with all your strength.' The second is this, 'You shall love your neighbour as yourself." No other commandment is greater than these."*

The Torah-teacher bowed his head respectfully and replied, *"Amen, Rabbi, you are right. You have truly said that Elohim is one, and beside him there is no other. And to love him with all the heart, and with all the understanding, and with all the strength, and to love one's neighbour as oneself — this is much more important than all these whole burnt-offerings and sacrifices."*

Yeshua looked steadily at him and a warm smile spread over his face.

"A wise response. You are not far from Elaha's kingly rule."

He looked around the crowd which had become very still.
"Anyone else got a question? No? Then let's turn to our prayers."

Followed by his trainees, Yeshua made his away across the
Outer Court, through the Beautiful Gate and into the Court of the
Women, where he stood for a long time, his hands raised in prayer.

Conversations[13]

After praying, Yeshua sat down at the side of the Court, next to
the Treasury. After a while, a woman, respectably dressed with
embroidery on her cloak and with bracelets on her arms, came up
to Yeshua.

"Shalom, Rabbi."

"Shalom, Miryam."

"Could I have a word in private?"

*"Surely, we'll go into this side room here. Tell me, how are you
doing?"*

"I'm fine, sad of course, but I'm fine."

"And your son, Yochanan Marcus?"

"Growing up too fast"

Yeshua chuckled as they disappeared from view.

Y'hudah Bar-Shim'on from K'riot looked after them suspiciously.

"What is he plotting now?" he asked T'oma.

"He's not plotting anything, you idiot," T'oma answered.

Y'hudah looked very uncertain, then seemed to come to a decision. He got up and ambled as unobtrusively as he could to the Hall of Polished Stone.

After a few minutes, Yeshua returned and said farewell to Miryam. He sat down next to the one of the thirteen big trumpet-shaped bronze donation boxes. Many wealthy men and women in highly-coloured striped and chequered cloaks came and theatrically tossed gold and silver coins into the metal mouths. Yeshua was idly watching everything going on. Suddenly he stiffened.

"See her?" he asked his group of trainees.

"Who?" "Which one?"

"That woman walking away, with the black cloak and shawl. The widow. I saw how much she put into the treasury box. Two farthings," he said admiringly.

"Two farthings? That's not much!"

"On the contrary. It's more than all the rest put in. Everyone else gave what they could afford. She gave what she couldn't afford, all that she had to live on. You may not have seen it, but the Holy One, blessed be he, certainly did."

The silver trumpets signalled the start of the evening sacrifice and Yeshua and his group stood up to pray.

At the end of the service they made their way to the North Gate. The sun was casting long shadows across the Outer Court, the tall Holy Place of the Temple dark against the light of the setting sun. *"Look, Rabbi, at these huge stones! How on earth did they get them here? And these magnificent buildings - they're incredibly beautiful. It must be the finest temple in the world!"*

Yeshua stopped dead and turned round to his excited trainees. *"Is that all you see? Big stones? Magnificent expensive buildings? I tell you solemnly, the time is coming when there will be not one stone left upon another. It will all be demolished."*

The trainees looked at him aghast - all apart from Y'hudah who had an expression of 'I told you so' on his face.

Yeshua looked each one in the face. Then, with a shrug, turned round and led the way down to the Kidron.

Notes for 13th Nisan/Wednesday

[1]Sources: Mark 12.13-37, 41-44

[2]Solomon's Portico was the wide covered colonnade on the long eastern side of the Outer Court, facing the Beautiful Gate which led into the Court of Israel. It had three rows of Corinthian columns, 40 feet high. After Pentecost, the first followers of 'the Way' regularly met there for prayer. (Acts 5.12).

[3]'Thank you' in Aramaic.

[4]The word 'Sadducees', or 'Tz'dukim', gives no clear idea to us today about this group. They were the top class in Israel, the religious and political leaders, so I have used the term 'Temple aristocrats'. They maintained that nothing should be believed or practised that was not specified in the written Torah, the first five books of the Bible. This included not accepting the idea of resurrection or angelic messengers. They represented the people to the Roman authorities. And were notably quarrelsome and corrupt.

[5]The quote used by the Temple aristocrats is from Deuteronomy 25.5-6. 'Moshe' is Hebrew for 'Moses'.

[6]The allusion to Tobiah's Sarah is to the Book of Tobit in the Apocrypha, Jewish scriptures written round about 200 BCE in Greek. The story tells how a demon which has killed all of Sarah's bridegrooms on their wedding night was defeated by Tobias by burning a fish's liver in the bedroom.

[7]The word 'angel', or 'angelos' in Greek, simply means messenger. It came to be commonly applied to God's messengers, his intermediaries between heaven and earth - God's realm and our human world. As Psalm 103.20 says:

> Bless the Lord, O you his angels,
> you mighty ones who do his bidding,
> obedient to his spoken word.

[8]'Torah' is normally translated (badly) as Law. It is in fact Law and Gospel for Jews, comprising the first five books from Genesis to Deuteronomy. Then Yeshua refers to 'the God of Abraham, the God of Isaac and the God of Jacob,' from Exodus 3.6.

[9]'Ha-Mashiach' reads in English as 'the Messiah'. It means the Anointed One, i.e. anointed by God to be king or high priest. (See Psalm 133.2). In the Old Testament only one person is called 'Messiah', and that is the Persian king Cyrus in Isaiah 45.1. Our own Queen Elizabeth was anointed at her coronation, so she could theoretically be called the same. The word is translated into Greek as Christos, in other words, Christ.

[10]'Ruach Ha-Kodesh' is Hebrew for the Holy Spirit. Ruach is a feminine noun, meaning wind or breath or some invisible, spiritual force. 'Kodesh' means 'Holy', with an underlying sense of weight.

[11]I have reversed the order of the two stories in Mark 12.28-37, the Torah-teacher's question and Jesus' comment on the Messiah as Son of David to make better dramatic sense.

[12]Hear, Israel, the Lord your God, the Lord is one.

[13]The episode of the woman Miryam is based on supposition. A key meeting place for the early church was the home of Mary, mother of John Mark, as in Acts 12.12. I assume she was a widow, because her husband is not mentioned. I also assume that her house was where the Last Supper took place. She had to meet Jesus in order to plan the secret sign which would lead the trainees to the right place to set up the meal. I further suppose that this private meeting was the last straw for Judas' suspicious mind.

14th Nisan

Passover eve

The Mount of Olives - Teaching

The Mount of Olives c. 1899
Public domain

Yeshua did not speak again as he led the group up the steep path to a cave near the top of the Mount of Olives[1]. He sat down, facing the translucent glow of the Temple in the dusk. One of the trainees used a flint and steel to set light to dry tinder, filled an oil lamp from a leather bottle and when the wick was alight, set down the lamp in the middle. The anxious faces of the trainees were now clearly visible, against a backdrop of deep shadows.

Two sets of brothers sat near Yeshua, Shim'on Kepha and Andreas, with Ya'akov and Yochanan Bar-Zavdai.

"Rabbi, tell us, when will this happen? What will be the signal that all these things are about to take place?"

Yeshua looked at each of them directly. They shifted uncomfortably. Yeshua called the rest of the twelve.

"Come nearer," he said. After the other eight had shuffled closer, he said, *"Watch out! Don't let anyone fool you! Many will come in my name, saying 'I'm the one!' And they will fool many people. When you hear the noise of wars nearby and the news of wars far off, don't become frightened. Such things must happen, but the end is yet to come. For people will fight each other, and nations will fight each other, there will be earthquakes in various places, there will be famines. This is but the beginning of the birth pains.*

"Now when you see 'the abomination that causes desolation'

standing where it has no right to be, that will be the time for those in Y'hudah to escape to the hills. If someone is on the roof, he must not go down and enter into his house to take any of his belongings; if someone is in the field, he must not turn back to get his coat. What a terrible time it will be for pregnant women and nursing mothers! Pray that it may not happen in winter.

"Now let the fig tree teach you its lesson. When its branches begin to sprout and leaves appear, you know that summer is approaching. In the same way, when you see all these things happening, you are to know that the time is near, right at the door. Yes! I tell you that this generation will not pass away before all these things happen.

"But you, watch yourselves! They will hand you over to the local Jewish councils, and you will be beaten up in their assembly halls, and on my account you will stand before governors and kings as witnesses to them. Now when they arrest you and bring you to trial, don't worry beforehand what to say. Rather, say whatever is given you when the time comes; for it will not be just you speaking but Ruach Ha-Kodesh.

"Brother will betray brother to death, and a father his child; children will turn against their parents and have them put to death; and everyone will hate you because of me. But whoever holds out to the end will be delivered.

"However, when that day and hour will come, no one knows - not the messengers of Elaha, not the Son, just the Father. So - stay alert! Be on your guard! For you do not know when that time will come."[2]

"Come on, my brothers, you look exhausted. Back to Beit-Anyah and get some sleep. You'll need it."

The trainees stretched their cramped legs and in anxious silence walked the half hour back, the moonlight clearly showing the path along the ridge back to their base.

Notes for 14th Nisan/Wednesday evening

[1]Up to the Persian conquest in 614, the Church in Jerusalem recalled Jesus' teaching on the End during Tuesday evening of Holy Week. This was done at the 4th century Church of the Olive Grove next to a cave which was traditionally the place where he taught his disciples about the destruction of Jerusalem and the second coming. There is 2nd century evidence that Jesus taught about the End in a cave on the Mount of Olives. The crusaders built a church on the site, dedicated to Jesus' teaching of the Lord's Prayer, hence the 'Church of Pater Noster'. The Byzantine ruins and the cave were rediscovered in 1910. The whole complex is very atmospheric and my favourite place in the whole of Jerusalem. I describe it in 'A Week of Prayer in Jerusalem'.

[2]Yeshua's talk is taken from Mark 13. It seems to be a compendium of sayings and teachings about the end times, collected together in one passage. I have used about half the material, and reordered it. The passages quoted are Mark 13.5-8, 14-18, 28-30, 9-13 (ed.), 32-34. The full account can be read in Mark 13, with parallel accounts in Matthew 24 and Luke 21. Jesus' talk here is based on David H Stern's translation, 'The Jewish New Testament.'

14th Nisan

Passover[1]

The Temple - a new opening

Palestinian sheep

Bethany

In Shim'on's house in Beit-Anyah, Yeshua and his trainees had breakfast of barley biscuits dipped in wine, the last time they would have regular bread for the next eight days. Then they went to the local mikveh[2] and bathed in preparation for Pesach. Outside the mikveh, Yeshua gathered his trainees round and spoke to them.

"Today is a great day," he told them, *"We're going to celebrate Elaha's great deliverance of our people, not just then but now. So we are going to eat Pesach in Yerushalayim itself. I'll need two of you to go and make all the preparations, the rest will come with me to the Temple. Any volunteers?"* They all volunteered, and Yeshua chose T'oma and Mattityahu.[3]

"Why not me, Rabbi?" asked Y'hudah Ish-K'riot. *"I know the city well."*

"No, Y'hudah, you stay with me. But you'll have to give Mattityahu enough money to pay for the lamb and all our provisions." With a rather bad grace, Y'hudah handed over several silver coins.

T'oma said, "Where are we going to eat Pesach, Rabbi? We've got nowhere in the city. And we don't know if the soldiers might not try to get you. We're safe here."

No, T'oma, we're going to fulfil the Torah. We are going to eat Pesach within the city. We'll all go to the Temple together, then you two go out through the Royal Porch to the Upper City.[4] *Just south of the City Market is one of the major cisterns. Wait there till you see a man going down to draw water and take it back up to his house."*

"A man! That'll be a turn up for the books!"

"Will he be wearing make-up as well?

"He must be a maid of all work!"

The trainees fell about laughing.

Yeshua smiled broadly. *"Yes, well, you won't mistake him, will you? Follow him, and ask at the house he goes into, 'Our teacher asks where is the guest room where he may eat Pesach with his trainees?' You will be shown a large guest room on the first floor, all set out for us. Check it's all prepared. The lady of the house will get anything else we need from the market during the morning. Then go back to the Temple, buy a lamb and have it sacrificed by a priest. When it's skinned, take it back and roast it over a spit in the courtyard of the house. That'll take five hours. We'll join you at dusk. And the rest of you, if we get separated, and I'm sure we will, we'll meet outside the Royal Porch after the evening prayers."*

They got to the Temple in time for the morning sacrifice. The whole of it, Court of Israel and the Outer Court, was heaving with pilgrims. A line of priests, dressed in white linen, created a pathway through the crowd from the North Gate to the Beautiful Gate for men to bring the lambs for sacrifice. Everyone wanted to have their lambs sacrificed on this special day, though in practice the sacrifices would have to continue all eight days of the Feast of Unleavened Bread. It was a real production line.[5]

The Temple

Yeshua was walking in his accustomed area in Solomon's Portico. Shortly after midday, Andreas and Philippos shouldered their way to him.

"Rabbi," Andreas said, *"Philippos has just told me that he met some Greeks from Antioch. They asked him if he was from Galilee and if he knew the prophet Yeshua. And if so, could he introduce them. He wasn't sure how to reply, because they're not from Y'hudah or the Galil, so he asked me. So, Rabbi, do you want us to bring them here so they can meet you?"*

It was rare for Yeshua to be taken aback, but this time he was. *"Well, well, well,"* he murmured to himself. *"So now it starts. Judaeans or goyim?"* he asked Philippos. *"Oh, Judaeans, Rabbi. We wouldn't meet goyim here, surely?"*

"I don't know, Philippos. We are in a new time. In fact the time has arrived for the son of man to come into his own. Amen amen, I tell you, if you want a seed to grow into a plant, you have to bury it in the ground and let it die. Death is the seed-bed of life. Let it die, and a harvest will come. So now is a time of grief and hope. Of hope and grief. What shall I say? Father, save me from this hour? No, my whole purpose was to come to this hour." He cried aloud, *"Father, may your holy will be carried out!"*

Strangely, out of the clear blue sky came a loud roll of thunder. The faces of everyone in the crowd, even the line of priests, looked up.

"You're wondering what that thunder portends? I'll tell you! It's the Holy One, blessed be he, telling you that his holy will has been carried out and will be carried out!"

Andreas said, "So, Rabbi, shall I get these Greeks and bring them here?"

"No, Andreas, it's time for the evening service. Let's go through the Beautiful Gate and pray. And then on to our Pesach supper."

Notes to 14th Nisan/Thursday day

[1]Sources: Mark 14.12-16, John 12.20-36

[2]A mikveh or mikveh is like a small bath-house for ritual washing. There was one in every important Jewish building.

[3]Mark does not name the two disciples who prepared the Passover. Luke tells us that it was Peter and John. I think if Peter had done it, Mark would have recorded it. So I have chosen two other disciples to be the volunteers.

[4]For me, one of the most powerful places in Jerusalem is the Church of St Mark, which has a subterranean room which they claim as the room where the Last Supper took place. I am inclined to believe them. That would put the house in the middle of the wealthy Upper City of 1st century Jerusalem, half way between the City Market and the Theatre. There were no springs of water in Jerusalem. Water came either from rainfall or aqueducts and was stored in cisterns. There were lots of them. My guess is that there was a major one near the City Market, and that is where the two trainees waited for the water-carrying man.

[5]Josephus tells us that at Passover 256,500 lambs were sacrificed in the Temple. Edersheim says that the Passover sacrifices started an hour early at 1.30. But that is impossible, because it takes four to five hours to roast a whole lamb. The sacrifices must have started as soon as the gates were opened. And sacrifices must have continued all the eight days of the Feast of Unleavened Bread.

15th Nisan

Passover Eve / First Day of Unleavened Bread[1]

The Upper City - Last Supper

Bread and wine at passover

A Guest Room, Upper City

The streets of the Upper City were busy with people moving between houses and slaves making last-minute preparations. Yeshua and his trainees came to a handsome house in the middle of the Upper City, not far from the High Priest's palace. The smell of roast lamb filled the air as they walked through the courtyard to the steps leading to the main guest room, a large upper room about 12 paces by 8^2 The tables had been beautifully set out with many oil lamps on stands around the room, as well as lamps on the tables. The tables were in the traditional three-sided arrangement, with Yeshua as the host reclining in the middle of the short table at one side, facing all but one of his trainees. Y'hudah Ish-K'riot reclined behind him and Yochanan directly in front of him. One of the household servants was just putting the finishing touches to the array of salads and side dishes they would enjoy before starting the meal proper. Yeshua said,

"Thank you for looking after us so well. I hope that the family and yourselves are well provided for?"

"Oh yes, thank you Rabbi. Your talmidim[3] had a really good lamb sacrificed for us all, as you saw downstairs."

"Yes indeed. Now go and join the rest of the household. Just bring us some lamb and the other requirements when you serve it for yourselves."

When the servant had left, the whole company sang the first of the great Hallel psalms:

> Praise the Lord!
> Praise, O servants of the Lord;
>   praise the name of the Lord.

After this, Yeshua took a deep breath and said, *"I have longed so much to eat this Pesach supper with you. It will be the last time I eat it before Elaha's kingly rule becomes a reality. There is suffering to come, but for now let's enjoy our celebration."* He started the informal eating of the appetisers by blessing the first cup of wine: *"Barukh ata Adonai Eloheynu, melekh ha'olam, bo're p'ri hagefen.[4] Share this among yourselves. I won't drink again of the grape until Elaha is king."* He passed it first to Y'hudah Ish-K'riot and then to Yochanan to share with the rest of the trainees.

The trainees did not know how to react, whether in anticipation or fear. The normal conversation over the appetisers was quite subdued. Each one said his own blessing over the particular appetisers, and over his own cup of wine. At the far corner a debate started between the two Ya'akovs as to who should volunteer to do the hand washing for everyone at table. Suddenly, all voices stopped as Yeshua stood up, took off his cloak, and went to the door. There he tied a linen towel around his waist, poured water from the large water jar into a bowl, and came back to the table. He knelt down at Y'hudah IshK'riot's feet, splashed a handful of water on his feet, and wiped them dry with the towel. Shock and embarrassment were on the faces of all the trainees. Yeshua continued along the line of feet of all the reclining men until he knelt before Shim'on Kefa. The big man tried to draw his feet up out of Yeshua's reach, exclaiming,

"Never, Rabbi! You shall never wash my feet!"

"Shim'on, if I don't wash your feet, you and I will have nothing in common with each other."

"Oh! If so, then please wash my hands and head as well!"

Yeshua smiled at Shim'on's impetuosity. *"You don't need all that, my friend. All of you have bathed today in preparation for Pesach. So if the dust is off your feet, the whole of you is clean. And you are clean. But not quite all of you."*
The trainees puzzled over this last remark as Yeshua continued the foot washing of all the twelve. At the end he stood up, put on his cloak and reclined in his place again.

"Do you realise what I have done? You call me Rabban and Maran[5], and you are correct. I am your teacher and master. So if I, your Rabban and Maran, have washed your feet, you also need to wash each other's feet. I have set you an example. It's for you to follow it through."[6]

A servant appeared bringing several plates piled with slices of roast lamb, together with the matzot - unleavened flatbread, bitter herbs and dishes of vegetables. He placed one of each dish in front of Yeshua for him to give the blessings. Yeshua took one of the large flatbreads and broke it in two while saying, *"Barukh ata Adonai Eloheynu, melekh ha'olam, hamotzi lehem min ha'aretz."[7]* Yeshua took a piece himself, reached back to give one to Y'hudah. As it was being passed down the line, Yeshua said, *"Take, each of you. This is my body. In the future, do this to remember me."* Anxious whispering filled the room. *"What's he saying? What does he mean? Bread-body? I don't understand."*

Yeshua stretched out his hand in blessing over the lamb, the flatbreads and the bitter herbs, and gave the explanations.

"This is the Passover sacrifice of the Lord, who passed over the houses of our fathers in Egypt when he smote the Egyptians.

"This is the dough of our ancestors, which did not have enough time to rise before the King of kings, the Holy One, blessed be he, appeared to them and redeemed them.

"These are the bitter herbs to remind us that the Egyptians embittered the lives of our forefathers in Egypt with hard labour."

Yeshua was silent for a while and his eyes filled with tears.

"Amen, amen, I say to you, one of you will betray me."

Shock and incredulity were on the face of all the trainees.

"What? No! That can't be true! We've been really careful, honestly. We've not told anyone where we are. The people love you, Rabbi, you're safe here during the feast, surely." After the first shock, each began to say, *"Rabbi, surely I won't be the one to be that stupid?"*

Yeshua said seriously, *"it's one who is sharing bread with me, one of our table fellowship. Didn't David himself say, 'Even my bosom friend in whom I trusted, who ate of my bread, has lifted the heel against me.'*[8]

Shim'on Kefa nodded at Yochanan and mouthed, *"Ask him who it is."* Yochanan leaned back towards Yeshua and whispered, *"Rabbi, who is it?'* Yeshua whispered back, *"The one I give the bread and charoseth to."*

He took a fragment of bread, dipped it in the mud-like charoseth, a mixture of fruit and nuts, leant back and offered it to Y'hudah, who received it with a muted *"I'm honoured, Rabbi."*

"If you need to do something, Y'hudah. now is the time to do it."

The trainee from Judaea hesitated. Yeshua had turned back and all Y'hudah saw was the back of his head. Gritting his teeth, he got up quickly and disappeared into the night.

"Hullo, where's Y'hudah gone off to?"

"Dunno. Some business or other. Get something for the festival.

Perhaps help some poor soul who's on his own tonight."

Yeshua visibly relaxed. *"Now my task is done. The will of Elaha has been accomplished, and will be accomplished. Lads, I'm going to be with you only a little longer, and you won't know where to find me. There's just one more order I have to give you. Love one another. I have loved you, trusted you, committed myself to you. You do the same for each other. Do I hear an Amen?"*

Heartfelt 'Amens' went round the room. But the meal had effectively drawn to an end, no one had much more appetite. Yeshua and his companions stood for the final thanksgiving prayer.[9]

"Let us give thanks."

The trainees responded, *"Blessed be the Name of the Lord from this time for evermore."*

Yeshua continued,

"Barukh ata Adonai Eloheynu, melekh ha'olam, who feeds the whole world with your goodness, with grace, with loving-kindness and with tender mercy. You give food to all beings, for your loving-kindness endures for ever. Through your great goodness food has never failed us. O may it not fail us for ever, for your great name's sake. Blessed are you, O Lord, who gives food to all.

"We thank you, Adonai Eloheynu, because you gave as a heritage to our fathers a desirable, good and pleasant land, and because you brought us forth, Adonai Eloheynu, from the land of Egypt and delivered us from the house of bondage; as well as for the covenant which you have sealed in our flesh; for your Torah which you have taught us; your statutes which you have made known to us; for the life, grace and loving-kindness which you have bestowed upon us, and for the food with which you constantly feed and sustain us every day, in every season and at every hour.

"For all this, Adonai Eloheynu, we thank you and bless you. Blessed be your name by the mouth of all living, continually and for ever, as it is written, 'And you shall eat and be satisfied, and you shall bless Adonai Eloheynu for the good land which he has given you. Barukh ata Adonai, for the food and the land."

Yeshua now took the final cup of wine, the cup of the blessing, and passed it on round the group. As it went round, he uttered these strange words:

"This cup of wine is the new covenant, the creation of a new community, sealed in my blood, shed for you."

One of the trainees almost choked while drinking when he heard this. They all stared at their Rabbi. What had he just said? What blood? The blood of the Temple sacrifices? A new covenant? What was all this about?

"Right, lads, time for the Hallel." The trainees started singing the five last psalms of the Hallel[9] as they went out of the courtyard into the quiet streets of the city.

> When Israel went out from Egypt,
>> the house of Jacob from a people of strange language,
> Judah became God's sanctuary,
>> Israel his dominion.

> Not to us, O Lord, not to us, but to your name give glory,
>> for the sake of your steadfast love and your faithfulness.
> Why should the nations say,
>> 'Where is their God?'

> I love the Lord, because he has heard
>> my voice and my supplications.
> Because he inclined his ear to me,
>> therefore I will call on him as long as I live.

Praise the Lord, all you nations!
Extol him, all you peoples!

O give thanks to the Lord, for he is good;
his steadfast love endures for ever!

The Walk to Gat Sh'manim

The group walked past Herod's palace and the Roman barracks, which doubled as the governor's residence when he was in Jerusalem, as now. They went through the gate next to the Hippichus Tower[10], part of the old king Herod's vast and extravagant palace with its three extraordinary towers. The gate was open, but heavily guarded, as normal during Pesach. The soldiers on guard duty did not challenge them, and kept their distance, in case any of them might be one of the dreaded revolutionary dagger-men. Shim'on called Zelotes looked quite ready to rumble, but he kept his feelings to himself and they passed through peacefully. They now followed the track around the outside of the city wall which would lead them to the Kidron valley.

Almost as soon as they had left the Hippichus Gate behind them, Yeshua stopped and stared at the small rocky hill to their left. The clear full moon lit it up, so that the sides gleamed like silver. On top of it half a dozen upright wooden posts stood silhouetted black against the night sky. Trees waiting for their next load of fruit - despairing wretches gasping out their lives in agony.

"Skull Hill," murmured Yeshua. *"How long, Adonai, how long?"* He turned to the worried trainees. *"I have to make you ready,"* he said. *"You have followed me all the way, through all the difficulties. I now declare to you that you will all sit with me at table when Elaha's kingly rule finally comes. But just for now, you will all desert me."*

"No, Rabbi, that's impossible - unthinkable!" each one exclaimed.

"Listen! It says in the Law and the Prophets, "'I will strike the shepherd, and the sheep will be scattered.'"[11] And no word of the Readings can stay unfulfilled. But take heart! After I have been raised, I will meet you in the Galil."[12]

Shim'on Kefa almost shouted his response. *"NEVER, Rabbi, never will I desert you! Even though everyone else runs away, I won't!*

"Really? Amen, amen, before we hear the second bugle signalling dawn, you will have said three times that you don't know me."

"No. NO! Even if it means dying with you! I'll never do it!"

"That goes for me too!" "And me." "You can rely on me, Rabbi." "I'll never leave you in the lurch!"

Yeshua looked sadly at the group of upset men. Then he focussed on Shim'on Kefa standing in the middle, looking as if he wanted to hit someone hard.

"Oh Shim'on, Shim'on, the Enemy has insisted on putting all of you through the shredder. But I have prayed for you, for you Shim'on, and when you are yourself again, encourage your brothers."

They continued their walk round the walls. When they had left the domineering walls of the Antonia Fortress behind then and were about to descend into the Kidron Valley, just before the steep descent, Yeshua turned to his trainees.

"Tell me, when we were in the Galil, did we have any problems with food and drink and shelter?"

"No, everyone was very welcoming, very generous."

"It's not going to be like that any more. If you've got a wallet, take it. If you've got a rucksack, that's ideal. If you've got a dagger to defend yourself, don't go out without it."

Shim'on Zelotes, proud to be of use for once, said, *"I've got one here."*

"Me too," said Taddai.

"Enough already!" exclaimed Yeshua. He turned and began the descent, shaking his head.

Notes to 15th Nisan/Thursday evening

[1] Sources: Mark 14.12-52, Luke 22.7-53, John 13, 18.1-11, 1 Corinthians 11.23-26, 'The Shape of the Liturgy' by Dom Gregory Dix, p.53, the Jewish 'Authorised Daily Prayer', compiled by Rabbi S Singer.

[2] My estimate of the dimensions of the 'Upper Room' below the Syrian Orthodox Church of St Mark.

[3] Talmidim' is Hebrew for 'disciple'. This is the only place I use this term instead of 'trainee'.

[4] Blessed are you, Lord our God, king of the universe, who creates the fruit of the vine.

[5] Rabban is a lofty title meaning Master. 'Maran' is Aramaic for 'Lord', as in 1 Corinthian's 16.22, 'Marana tha' - 'Lord, come.' The ordinary word for lord or master is Mar. Maran indicates a supreme lord.

[6] The story of the foot-washing only occurs in John. Did it happen? If it did, why did the other three gospels leave it out? Perhaps it was just too embarrassing. Within a couple of months of Jesus' resurrection and the gift of the Spirit at Pentecost, the Twelve were saying, *"'It is not right that we should neglect the word of God in order to wait at tables."* (Acts 6.2)

We don't know exactly when the foot washing occurred. It may have happened after the blessing of the bread during the Passover meal itself. I have placed it in this earlier position because I think it makes more sense there.

[7] Blessed are you, Lord our God, who brings forth bread from the earth.

⁸Psalm 41.9

⁹The Hallel comprised Psalms 113 to 118. Psalm 113 was sung before the meal, the rest after it. The first verse or two of each of the six psalms are quoted here, in the New Revised Standard Version (NRSV) translation.

Psalm 118 in particular was seen by Jesus as a prophecy pointing to himself.

¹⁰The remains of one of the three towers built by Herod today forms the base of the Tower of David or Citadel, next to the Jaffa Gate. It might be the Phasael Tower, named after Herod's brother who committed suicide in prison, or the Hippichus Tower, named after Herod's great friend, who managed to die a natural death. The third tower was named after Herod's beloved wife Mariamne, executed at a time of jealous rage, and buried nearby.

¹¹Zechariah 13.7

¹²A serious puzzle to the Christian story is that Jesus promises to meet them in Galilee but after the resurrection turns up in Jerusalem. Rabbi Pinchas Lapide, in his book 'The Resurrection of Jesus' suggests that 'Galil' is a generic word meaning 'region'. So Galilee is actually Galil ha Goyim - region of Gentiles. Galil Yerushalayim is the region around Jerusalem. That would be a neat solution!

15th Nisan

First Day of Unleavened Bread[1]

Gethsemane and Palace of Annas

17th century olive press, Croatia.
Miomir Magdevski. Greyscale of colour photo
Licensed under Creative Commons Attribution
Share Alike 4.0 International licence

The Olive Grove

When they got to Gat Sh'manim, Yeshua went through the gate in the low stone wall, followed by the trainees.

"It's late, why aren't we going straight to Beit Anyah?" grumbled Mattatyahu to Ya'akov BenChalfai.

"We've got to wait for Y'hudah. We don't want him being picked up by the police."

Yeshua said to the trainees, *"I know you're tired. Have a break and relax for the time being. Shim'on Kefa, Ya'akov and Yochanan, come with me. I need to pray."*

They walked past the mikveh[2] and the large stone olive press, with the wooden beam for donkeys to turn the giant millstone. On the other side, Yeshua said, *"Stay here. I'm going on a little further."* He went another fifty paces into the shade of the olive grove and crouched down, his head in his hands. *"Abba, Abba,"* he cried, *"you can do anything. Take away this cup of suffering. Deliver me from my enemies. Oh my help, come quickly to my aid! But. But. Your will, Abba. Your will be done. Your will be done."* He slowly got up and walked back through the orchard. The night was completely silent apart from the coo-ick of a distant nightjar. All three trainees were asleep, and no sound came from the other group. Yeshua, shook them awake. *"Come on, my brothers, try to stay awake. I want you to be with me tonight. It's hard for me."*

He went back to the former spot and prayed in the same way, but when he returned they were out like a light again. Once more he woke them up, but the third time he let them sleep. Until there was a noise at the entrance gate of the olive grove.

"Quickly! Wake up! The traitor is here!" The three trainees stood up groggily and there was a confused noise as the other trainees woke up and realised that they were confronted by a posse of Temple guards and Roman soldiers[3]. They scattered among the olive trees, but stopped when they realised they were not being pursued. They realised that the one leading the armed mob with their lanterns and flaming torches was their friend Y'hudah. They were completely confused.

Yeshua strode forward past the olive press into the light of the lanterns.

"Are you looking for someone?" he asked the group of men armed with truncheons and swords. Their self-confidence was shaken and there was a pregnant pause. Then Y'hudah came forward, kissed Yeshua on the cheek and said, *"Shalom, Rabbi"*. *"My friend, do you betray the son of man with a kiss?"* asked Yeshua quietly. As if on a signal, the armed crowd surged forwards and two of them grabbed Yeshua by the arm. Shim'on Zelotes[4] shouted *"NO!"*, pulled out his dagger and slashed at the head of one of the men holding Yeshua. The man moved to get out of the way and then screamed as his ear was almost severed.

"STOP IT!" shouted Yeshua and there was a stunned silence. Yeshua held the injured man's head in both hands for a moment. The man stood there dazed, then staggered back, touching this ear, not quite believing that the bleeding had stopped.

Yeshua took a deep breath, then spoke strongly.

"Are you really coming to get me in the middle of the night with billy clubs and swords? Do you really think I'm a dangerous bandit? Every single day this week I have been in the Temple teaching, praying, talking. No one laid a finger on me then. But I guess that darkness suits you. Only, let these men go."

The Roman decurion[5] shouted, *"Arrest him!"* The group of Roman soldiers and Temple guards ran forward and grabbed him, and some started after the trainees who scattered in fear. One young man was spotted because the white sheet he had wrapped himself in gave him away, but he wriggled out of it and ran off naked. The decurion shouted again, *"Come back, men, we've got the guy we want."* The soldiers handed Yeshua over to the Temple guards who tied his wrists tight behind his back, and pushed him roughly up the road back to Yerushalayim.

The Palace of the High Priest Annas[1,6]

It was now the middle of the night, with the moon high overhead. The posse with their prisoner marched back up the hill, past the Pool of Bethesda, and up to the Antonia Fortress. Here the Roman officer and soldiers left them. The Temple guards took their prisoner through the gate leading to the grand Hasmonean palace. Part of it was the palace of Anan the senior High Priest, father-in-law to the official High Priest Kayafa. Yeshua was marched into its courtyard. After a lengthy pause with men running into and out of the palace, Yeshua was taken into the main hall.

An imposing elderly white-bearded man was seated in the middle of various officials and servants. This was Anan whom the Romans had replaced as high priest over twenty years before, There was no sign of a secretary to take down evidence or of any of the members of the Great Council.

"So, Yeshua Ish-Natzaret, the preacher from Galil haGoyim, I am glad to see you, though obviously in unfortunate circumstances. You have made quite a name for yourself over this Pesach. Now, you are here on your own. Perhaps you can tell us something about those who follow you. I believe that they are almost all from the Galil ha Goyim, is that true?"

Yeshua was silent.

"I can understand your wish not to incriminate any of your friends, but as the Great Council, we have a responsibility to safeguard the festival. It could lead to disaster if there was anything like a riot to happen. So please tell us, who are your close followers and where can we find them? It's important, even if only for their protection."

Again, no response.

"Well now, perhaps we can move to a different subject. Your teaching, now. I fear I have not had the opportunity to hear you in person, but as I understand it, you have made certain inflammatory statements which seem designed to turn people against us priests and leaders of the Temple. And yet the worship of the Temple is surely the heart, the beating heart of our nation, both here in Palestine and indeed all over the known world. Tell me, if you are a prophet, as some apparently claim, what is it you have said?"

At last Yeshua spoke.

"I have taught every day in the Temple throughout this week. Ask those who heard me."

A Temple guard on his left backhanded him hard on the right cheek, then gripped his jaw tightly in his hand.

"Is this how you answer back our high priest? Show some bloody respect!"

Yeshua shook his face free from the guard and said very deliberately,

"If I've spoken wrongly, make your statement as a witness. If not, why did you hit me?"

Anan intervened. *"Officer, I fully understand your frustration, but it won't help anyone if we allow this Galilean to rile us. As you know, my son-in-law Kayafa has been the official high priest for almost twenty years. He has enough experience to know how to deal with people who cause trouble. I only thought that we might be able to come to some more peaceable arrangement, unofficially."* He turned his attention to Yeshua. *"So, preacher, are you not going to tell us what you have been speaking to the pilgrims here in Yerushalyim about?"*

Again, Yeshua was silent.

"Ah well, no one can say I didn't try. You'd better send him down to my son-in-law. He has a secure prison cell, small but certainly adequate for our preacher. Take him outside and look after him while I write a note to Yosef."[7]

Four guards walked Yeshua out of the hall and tripped him up, so he fell flat on the marble pavement. They all laughed.

"Hey, guys, we can have a bit of fun with our prophet. Someone put a blindfold on him."

They hauled him to his feet, wrapped a cloth over his eyes and pushed his back against a wall. One punched him hard in the stomach.

"Come on, prophet, tell me what my name is. Don't know? Maybe this will help." Another punch.

"He's a bit sleepy, ain't he? Maybe a slap will wake him up." Two slaps, left and right, followed. *"Come on, prophet, tell us the winner in the chariot race tomorrow, I could do with some winnings."* Silence. *"Ah, you spoilsport. Take that!"* A fist struck his chin. *"Hey, go easy Matt, don't knock him out! We don't want to have to carry him through the city."*

The guards suddenly stood to attention and one of them hurriedly undid the blindfold. The high priest's secretary came out to them with a papyrus scroll.

"Here, take this to Kayafa with the prisoner. And don't loiter."

The guards marched Yeshua through the large courtyard, lit by the flickering flames of a charcoal brazier. Just then the bugle call sounded from the Antonia, marking the start of the late night watch.[8] Yeshua's gaze rested for a moment on the grief-stricken face of Shim'on Kefa standing at the back of the mixed crowd of servants and soldiers, curious about the fate of the northern preacher. Yeshua's face remained impassive as he was hustled out of the front archway into the quiet dark streets of the Upper City.

Prison

The little group walked past opulent mansions and the City Market to the imposing pyramid of the Tomb of David, directly opposite the High Priest's palace. The guards took every opportunity to prod Yeshua with their truncheons, *"Come on, prophet, keep up."*

Kayafa's palace was a hive of activity. Flaming torches at the main entrance lit up the street, with more of them as well as charcoal braziers in the courtyard. It was crowded with uniformed troops and household servants, hurrying on various errands. The guards from Anan's palace handed Yeshua over to Kayafa's captain of security. The captain took Yeshua personally down a flight of steps, cut the cords tying his wrists, pushed him down a couple steps into a small windowless dungeon[9], banged the door shut and bolted it. Yeshua was left in pitch darkness in a bare stone cell with rotting straw underfoot. He did not sleep. He spent the time recalling the prayers of David:

'Save me, O God, for the waters have come up to my neck.
I sink in deep mire, where there is no foothold;
I have come into deep waters, and the flood sweeps over me.
I am weary with my crying; my throat is parched.
My eyes grow dim with waiting for my God.[10]

A couple of hours later, the door opened, Yeshua's wrists were tied again in front him and he was taken up to the inner courtyard. Night was beginning to lighten. You could see the black of buildings against the slightly lighter blue-black of the night sky. Two guards stood next to Yeshua and watched the comings and goings of the palace servants, priests in white tunics and Torah-teachers in black cloaks. The bugle call from the Antonia for the early morning watch could just be heard as a servant came out and told the captain to bring the prisoner to the small hall at the back of the palace complex.

Notes on 15th Nisan/Thursday night

[1]Sources: John 18.12-24

[2]Archaeologists have recently discovered a mikveh or ritual bath house in Gethsemane. A reasonable assumption is that it was for the workers in the olive press so that the oil they produced would be ritually clean and so able to be used in the Temple.

[3]John's gospel specifies that Jesus' arrest was carried by a mixed cohort of both Roman soldiers and Temple police.

[4]Only John says that it was Simon Peter who used the dagger. I think if it had been, his name would have been in at least one of the other gospels. I think it may have been the other Simon, whose name indicates that he had been a Zealot, a revolutionary nationalist.

[5]My guess is that the Roman officer at the arrest was a decurion, similar to an NCO (non-commissioned officer), in charge of a squad of ten to twenty men.

[6]The pattern of events incorporating the various trials of Jesus is highly disputed. Only John mentions the trial under Annas/Ananias and barely mentions the trial under Caiaphas. Mark (and Matthew) say that the trial under Caiaphas was at night, which was illegal. Luke says it was in the early morning. The key seems to me that there were two high priests at that time. Annas, who ruled from 6 to15 AD and his son-in-law Caiaphas who ruled from 18 to 36 AD. Luke calls them both high priests in Luke 3.2, both being appointed by Roman governors and anointed. I take John's account seriously, and it makes sense. They had to secure Jesus and hold on to him until there could be a legal trial under Caiaphas at first light. The palace of Annas was conveniently near the gate where they would have brought Jesus through, and an unofficial questioning was an ideal opportunity to try and get a damaging admission from him. I think that Annas was asked to question Jesus as a delaying measure, not just so that the trial with the Sanhedrin would be legal, but to give Caiaphas time to scrabble round, call the Sanhedrin together and try to find useful witnesses. I follow Luke's account which does not have a night-time questioning by Caiaphas. That all happens in the legal trial at 6.00 AM.

It was not abnormal to rise and start the day while it was still dark. Mary Magdalene did so (John 20.1), Jesus did so (Mark 1.35), and the Temple priests did so daily in order to draw lots for the various tasks to be done before the day started. Dawn was 6.30, so first light would have been at 6.00.

[7]Yosef Ben Kayafa, known by his second name, Caiaphas.
The Hebrew form of Annas was Anan or Ananias.

[8]Jesus warned Simon Peter that he would deny his master three times before the cock crowed twice. That seems to refer to more than the ordinary domestic roosters. William Barclay in his commentary on Mark says that when the Roman sentry guard was changed, a bugle call was made, called in Latin 'gallicinium', meaning cock crow. This would have been the routine in the Antonia fortress, overlooking Jerusalem.

These bugle calls would have been at 6pm, 9pm, midnight, 3am and 6am. Barclay assumes that midnight was the first bugle call and 3am the second. That makes sense if Peter's denial took place during the questioning of Jesus in the palace of Annas, as in John's gospel.

[9]Archaeologists have found a dungeon in what is assumed was the palace of Caiaphas.

[10]Psalm 69.1-3. The Early Church found this psalm to be a remarkable prophecy of the suffering of their Messiah.

15th Nisan

First Day of Unleavened Bread[1]

The Palace of Caiaphas

Model of Caiaphas' Palace

Two guards stood on either side of Yeshua with the captain alongside. The hall they were in was not large enough to hold the whole of the Great Council.[2] The Hall of Polished Stone in the Temple was their official location. But there was plenty of room for the two dozen Temple aristocrats and leading priests to sit on stools in a shallow semi-circle along the long wall of the room with the High Priest in the centre.[3] The captain smiled grimly to himself. He recognised that most of them were members of just six priestly families. *"The man's not got a chance,"* he thought to himself.

Kayafa, an imposing man in his mid-fifties, tall and with a full black beard, stood up and addressed Yeshua.

"Prisoner, you have been arrested on a number of charges. Witnesses will be brought in for us to consider the evidence. But first, your name?"

Yeshua was silent.

"Ach, is this your stupid game? Can anyone here witness to the name of the prisoner?"

"I met him in the Temple, when he ridiculed us priests and Torah-teachers. His name is Yeshua Bar-Yosef."

"I believe he is normally called Yeshua Ish-Natzeret, because that is his home village."

"He also goes by the name of Yeshua Bar-Miryam, for reasons we can only guess at."

A ripple of laughter ran round the hall. Kayafa spoke again.

"Well, Yeshua, we can only speculate why you need so many names. It doesn't seem to me a very honest procedure. But I suppose it is not illegal, so let us quickly pass on. Bring in the first witness."

Kayafa sat down. A man wearing an embroidered cloak and with an avaricious face entered.

"Your name?"

"El'ichud Bar-Z'khariyah, your Grace."

"Welcome. What charges do you bring against the prisoner?"

"For over twenty years I have been faithfully changing defiled money into sacred coinage so that worshippers can properly buy their sacrifices. No one in authority has ever complained about my business. But four days ago, this Galilean stormed into the sacred Temple, threw over my table and the tables of my colleagues and ordered us to leave. I only did so because of the scores of his supporters who were frankly threatening, and I did not want our holy house to be desecrated by violence. I lost a great deal of honestly acquired money through this mountebank!"

"So - your charges are incitement to violence, destruction of property and desecration of the Temple."

"Yes, your Grace. And I have several friends outside wishing to make the same charges."

"Yeshua, how do you plead to these charges?"

Silence.

"Thank you El'ichud. Please withdraw, while we discuss your evidence."

When the merchant had left, Kayafa addressed the Council.

"What the merchant said is undoubtedly true, but it will hardly serve our purpose. The most we could sentence this pretended prophet to is a flogging and time in prison. With thousands of his fellow-Galileans here in the city we have to act decisively, and fast. They will be beginning to gather in the Temple in a couple of hours. Do you agree?"

All murmured their assent.

"Very well. Call the next witness."

A Torah-teacher entered with dignity.

"My name is Yannai Ben-Mattat. I accuse Yeshua Ish-Natzeret of political sedition."

"When did you witness this?"

"Four days ago, late morning."

"Tell us of the incident."

"I was part of a delegation challenging Yeshua about his high-handed behaviour in seizing control of the Outer Court, abetted by his fellow Galilean pilgrims. He gave a very slippery response, which we decided, for reasons of public order, to let go. But I stayed behind to hear how he dealt with a most serious issue, namely the payment of the imperial taxes. His reply, on the face of it was clever: 'Give to Caesar what belongs to Caesar, and to Elohim what belongs to Elohim'. However, as anyone who has done any study of the Torah and Haftorah knows, the Holy One, blessed be he, has taken Yisrael as his own possession. So what the Galilean said was

in effect a call for bloody revolution. We know that the well-being of Yisrael at this point in time means to accept and to pray for the Empire which has authority over the whole Syrian region, just as the Holy One, blessed be he, spoke through the mouth of Yirmeyahu."[4]

Many of the Council members were starting to look bored, impatient or confused. One of them whispered to his neighbour. *"D'you think this will stand up?"* His neighbour shrugged. Kayafa smiled amiably at the Torah-teacher.

Kayafa addressed Yeshua. *"So, prisoner, do you support the refusal of paying taxes to the Empire? Do you reject the word of Adonai as spoken by the prophet Yirmeyahu?"*

Silence

"Ah well, Yannai Ben-Mattat, we are obliged to you for your great learning, which I for one appreciate. It certainly is something that the Governor, should this matter come before him, which Heaven forbid, would take cognisance of. But I think if we pursued it here at this moment, our discussion could last all eight days of the Feast. Thank you, Yannai. Perhaps the Council could express their thanks in the traditional way?" A scattering of applause rang round the hall, and the Torah-teacher left with a self-satisfied smile on his face. *"Call another witness."*

A man in a shabby cloak and a face which portrayed a history of alcohol entered, clearly overawed by the row of powerful gentlemen seated facing him.

"Your name?"

"Tolmai Bar-Y'hudah, your Honour. But people call me Tol."

"Well, Tol, what can you tell us about this man?"

"He's a wizard, your honour! A sorcerer! He's been in Egypt and that's where he learnt all his powerful spells.[5] Everyone knows it!"

"Have you met him before?"

"No. No. I wouldn't. I don't get mixed up in anything like that."

"So how do you know that what you claim is true?"

"Everybody in Yerushalayim knows it! It's common knowledge!"

Kayafa sighed and with a trace of impatience said, "Thank you, Tol. Sadly we won't be able to use your testimony. We can't rely on hearsay evidence. But clearly your heart is in the right place. So thank you, you may withdraw. And guards, do give our friend a cup wine for his trouble."

The secretary said, "There are two other witnesses, your Grace, Temple guards."

"Excellent, show the first of them in."

A tall man in the uniform of a Temple guard entered, removed his helmet and marched to the front where he stood to attention.[6]

"What is your name, guard, and what is your accusation against the prisoner?"

"My name is Avraham Bar-L'vi. I am a member of the Temple Guard. I accuse the prisoner of wizardry and sacrilege."

"What day did the event happen which you are accusing him of?"

"Four days ago, your Grace."

"And at what time?"

127

"Shortly before midday."

"Please continue with your accusation."

"I was on duty in the Temple when this man Yeshua caused a riot which drove the authorised traders out of the Temple. After he and his Galilean followers had occupied the Outer Court, some of the merchants, justly angered, asked him to show what prophetic sign he could give to justify his action. I heard his reply. He said, 'I will destroy this Temple made with hands and build another, made without hands.'"

A shocked murmur went up from everyone in the hall. Kayafa allowed himself a small smile, as he ordered the other Temple guard to come in.

He marched in and stood to attention next to his comrade.

"What is your name, guard, and what is your accusation against the prisoner?"

"I'm Shim'on Bar-Yitzchak. I accuse the prisoner of wizardry."
"What day did the event happen which you are accusing him of?"
"Four days ago, your Grace."

"And at what time?"

"Shortly before midday."

"Please continue with your accusation."

"Four days ago I was on duty in the Temple when the prisoner started a riot and drove all the traders out of the Temple. When he was challenged about his actions, I heard him say, 'I am able to destroy this holy place and build it again in three days.'"

One of the Council members, one of the youngest there, only about forty years old, raised a question.

"Did he say that he would rebuild it without using hands?"

"I don't remember him saying that. He did say he'd rebuild it in three days."

The other guard interrupted.

"No, he definitely said he'd do it without hands."

"I don't think so."

An older council member spoke up.

"Words of wizardry are not the same as wizardry. He could be deluded or be mentally ill."

Kayafa was visibly annoyed.

"Thank you guards, your evidence has been helpful. Have a cup of wine each on your way out." He turned his gaze onto Yeshua. *"We have heard these two honourable witnesses. It is clear that that whatever the exact words, you said that if the Temple were to be destroyed - may it never come to pass - you would rebuild it in three days. That is a clear claim to magical powers. So - do you practise the dark arts? Are you a wizard, or something worse?"*

Silence.

A streak of sunlight hit one side of the hall. The sun had risen. A faint sound of silver trumpets announced the morning sacrifice of the lamb was about to take place and the great gates of the Temple to open. Time was going on. Soon the Temple would be thronged with pilgrims. When news of Yeshua's arrest become known, anything could happen.

Kayafa looked straight at the calm figure of Yeshua in front of him, noting his erect stature, his fearless gaze, as if he, Yeshua, was the one in authority here in the hall - here in Yerushalayim - here in Yisrael.

"Maybe this will work," Kayafa said to himself. With great dignity, he stood up. You could have heard a pin drop. Kayafa and Yeshua looked straight into each others' eyes. Kayafa said quietly, almost conversationally,

"Yeshua Ish-Natzaret, are you Ha-Mashiach - the Anointed - the Son of the Blessed One?"

There was a pause and everyone held their breath.

Yeshua said, equally quietly in Aramaic, *"Ena ena - I am[7]."*

The council chamber erupted into shocked cries from the whole assembly. Yeshua's voice rose above them all. *"AND YOU WILL SEE THE SON OF MAN SEATED AT THE RIGHT HAND OF THE MOST HIGH AND COMING ON THE CLOUDS OF HEAVEN!"*

Kayafa gestured for the noise to abate and then theatrically tore the top half of his blue silk tunic in two.

"You have heard the blasphemy? That such things should be uttered in Yisrael! What is your verdict?"

"ISH MAVET!"[8] *"DEATH,"* was the almost unanimous shout.

"My lord", whispered the secretary, *"Is this strictly legal? Blasphemy means stoning. That might be difficult in a city full of pilgrims."*

"I know. Don't fear, he said he was Ha-Mashiach - God's anointed. That's a political claim. We'll take him over to the Romans. I had a word with Pilatus last night. Sometimes even the Romans have their uses."

Out in the courtyard of Kayafa's palace, the guards waited with Yeshua for the delegation of priests and Temple aristocrats to assemble.

"By the sacred altar, this is a special day. It's not often we get to arrest Ha-Mashiach! You've got a nerve, mate, a provincial from the Galil!"

"Careful, Yitzchak, or he may slay you with the rod of his mouth!"

The guards fell about laughing and started a game of each slapping him on the cheek, left, right, left, right. Yeshua stood impassively throughout. After a few minutes the captain intervened.

"That's enough fun for now, lads. Untie his hands and retie them behind his back. He's a condemned prisoner now, right?" The guards tied rough cords round Yeshua's wrists. The doors from the council hall opened. The captain ordered, *"Attention, men. Here's the High Priest. Get ready to march the prisoner to the governor's headquarters."*

Notes on 15th Nisan/Friday morning – the Trial under Caiaphas

[1]Sources: Mark 14.55-65, 15.1, Luke 22.66-71, 1 Peter 2.21-23

[2]Where did the trial under Caiaphas happen? There are two contenders: The Temple, specifically in the Hall of Polished Stone where full meetings of the Sanhedrin, which I call the Great Council, took place; and the Palace of Caiaphas, the High Priest, which had a dungeon, recently discovered, and a smaller hall which would not accommodate all the Sanhedrin, but would certainly be enough for a quorum of 23 to hear the case against Jesus. And Caiaphas could easily arrange for a picked body of Council members and of potential witnesses to come to his palace at night ready for daybreak. In the Temple it would be more awkward, with numerous gates and gatekeepers to organise etc.

[3]The Mishnah (c. 200 AD) gives the quorum for a meeting of the Sanhedrin as twenty three.

[4]Yirmeyahu is the Hebrew form of Jeremiah

[5]This is an accusation levelled at Jesus in the Talmud, c.300 AD

[6]The account of the two temple guards giving testimony against Jesus is taken partly from the brilliant series of radio plays 'The Man Born to be King' by Dorothy Sayers (1941), supplemented by court procedures recorded in the Mishnah, c. 200 AD. I cannot recommend Dorothy Sayers' book highly enough. It is very dramatic. You can get it on Amazon.

[7]'Ena ena' is the Aramaic for 'I am', and are the words used in the ancient Syriac version of Marks' gospel. It corresponds to the Hebrew 'Ehyeh'. "Ehyeh" is the first word in God's reply to Moses at the burning bush 'I am who I am', (Exodus 3.14). In the next verse the name given is 'Yahweh' (probably) or Jehovah (traditionally). It means 'He is'.These words stopped being pronounced about a hundred years before Jesus' birth. The Mishnah, c. 200 AD, a collection of rabbinic judgements, said, "He who pronounces the Name with its own letters has no part in the world to come!"

[8]'Ish Mavet' - man of death - was the death sentence (Talmud).

15th Nisan

First Day of Unleavened Bread[1]

The Praetorium and Herod's Palace

Praetorium/Governor's headquarters

The Governor's Headquarters/Praetorium[1]

Kayafa had changed into a white silk tunic and a royal blue cloak, impressively ornamented with gold, jewels and pearls. He walked at the head of a group of six priests and Temple aristocrats in their best white linen, followed by the guards marching ahead of and behind Yeshua. They walked the short distance along Market Street. The street was beginning to fill with people, all gawping at the unusual procession taking place - and, amazingly, on the First day of Unleavened Bread. Directly opposite the Market Square was the heavily fortified entrance to the two palaces. The guard on duty saluted Kayafa respectfully and sent a messenger to the procurator's HQ. The group turned right into the central space between the two palaces, the size of two football fields, and walked to the Praetorium at the end.[2] The group halted in front of the 25-foot-wide porch leading to the Governor's residence. The enormous Mariamne tower loomed overhead, which Herod the Great had erected in memory of his beloved wife Mariamne, whom he had had executed. The early morning sun made the white marble blaze like a beacon, and lit up the top two stories of Pilatus' headquarters.

A slave came out, bowed respectfully and said that the governor would be out in a minute. A couple of slaves brought out a gilded wooden chair with sloping arms and carved insignia of Rome and a bronze table with three legs, and placed them in the middle of the porch. Another slave brought in a silver goblet and a small jug of wine. A secretary brought in papyrus, reed pen and ink, a clay shorthand tablet and a wooden writing board.

Pontius Pilatus, every inch a military man, strode out of the Praetorium's gateway, wearing a short white toga over a white tunic with two narrow vertical purple-red stripes.[3] He walked over to Kayafa and shook his hand.

"Xairé,[4] your Grace."

"Xairé, Excellency."

Pilatus sat down and looked enquiringly at the high priest.

"Well, High Priest, I assume this is the person we have spoken about. Perhaps you can enlighten me about the exact charges against him."

"Excellency, I assure you we would not have bothered you at this early hour had it not been a matter of some gravity. I have just come from a meeting of the Great Council - small, but quorate - and it was our almost unanimous decision that this man needs to suffer the supreme penalty of being a threat to the Empire. To deal with the prisoner is in our view essential to keeping good order in the land."

"High Priest, I don't need you to tell me how to maintain order. What I do need is for you to tell me why he is such a threat."

"Of course, Excellency. Brother Sila, please be so kind as to summarise the findings of the Council."

"Absolutely, your Grace. Excellency. This man has been a disturber of the peace for many months. He even sacrilegiously brought violence into the Temple itself only four day ago."

"I am aware of that. I do get daily reports from my officer in the Antonia. He reports that the Temple since that incident has been unusually peaceful."

"Yes, Excellency, but he does make inflammatory statements. For example, only two days ago he made a coded comment inviting people to stop paying their imperial taxes."

"Coded? In what way coded?"

The priest Sila blushed with embarrassment and could not think of a reply.

"Prisoner, perhaps you can enlighten me. What were these coded comments about not paying the imperial taxes?"

Yeshua looked straight at Pilatus but said nothing. Kayafa interjected, *"Excellency, we found this self-same stubbornness when we in the Great Council were interrogating him. Carry on, brother Sila."*

"Excellency, he has created upset all over the province. He does not keep the Shabbat but insists on carrying on his alleged healing campaigns which simply sow division and create unrealistic expectations..."

"Priest, I am deeply uninterested in your religious disputes. I shall therefore..."

"Excellency, I apologise for interrupting you, but the most serious charge has only just now come to light. In the meeting of the Great Council he claimed to be - er – 'Ha Mashiach...'"

Kayafa broke in smoothly.

"Xristos, Excellency, the Anointed. It is a special royal title for us. Judas the Galilean who raised a revolt in the year of the census under

the noble legate Quirinius, made a similar claim. His insurrection had to be put down by force with considerable loss of life."

"So, High Priest, tell me in plain words what 'Xristos' means to you and your people."

"The best I can say is, 'Basileus Iudaeōn' - the King of the Jews.

"Really? The King of the Jews? All of them? Here? Alexandria? Rome? All right, I now have something to ask him. Ieesoo[5] - are you the King of the Jews?"

Yeshua stayed silent, simply looked calmly at the governor.

"Don't you have anything to say about the accusations these worthy gentlemen had made?"

Again silence.

One of the priests broke in excitedly.

"Excellency, you'll never get anything out of him. But in fact he has spread his message of civil disruption all over the province. Not just here in Yerushalayim, but especially in the Galil where he comes from."

Kayafa winced and muttered under his breath, "Idiot!"

Pilatus looked pleased for the first time that morning.

"Really? Well, our colleague Herod Antipas, the ruler of Galilee, is of course here for Passover, and is opposite. I suggest that you take him to him." He turned to the secretary.

"Take down this note.

'Pontius Pilatus, procurator of Judaea and Samaria, to the
honourable Herod Antipas, Tetrarch of Galilee and Peraea.

Xairé. I wish you health and good fortune.

I have just finished questioning a prisoner brought to me by the
high priest Caiaphas. His name is Iēsous and he has been accused
of disturbing the peace in various ways, or rather of disturbing our
good friends of the Sanhedrin. Apparently, he has claimed publicly
to be the Xristos - the Anointed - about which I know little. However,
in my questioning I have discovered that he is in fact a citizen of
Galilee and therefore comes under your jurisdiction. I am sending
him over to you for your decision on his future. Please give my
regards to your lady wife Herodias.

The eighteenth year of Tiberius Caesar, the seventh day of Aprilios.'

Now soldier, take the note along with his Grace and the prisoner
to Herod."

As the group of priests, guards and Yeshua crossed the enormous
mosaic piazza to the palace entrance at the other end, Kayafa
tapped the captain on the shoulder.

"Go back to my residence and get your men to round up some
reliable people. Get them to the Market Square, ready to come
in here when they're allowed. We need to ensure that we have
sound citizens who can make a noise. I suggest you start in the
merchants' quarter." The captain saluted and marched back to the
High Priest's palace to take the necessary action.

The Palace of Herod Antipas

The escort party came to a halt outside the porch leading to
the palace of Herod Antipas. A peacock squawked angrily at
being disturbed and stalked off to a far corner. The chamberlain
greeted Kayafa and the priests respectfully and ushered them

into the main reception room, lined with gleaming bronze shields, breastplates and crossed swords. Herod Antipas, a corpulent man in his mid-fifties, wearing a purple tunic held together with a gold and jewelled brooch, sat in a wicker armchair, a bowl of dusty fruit on a table next to him.[6]

"Ah, my dear Kayafa, how good to see you. Do excuse me for not getting up, but life takes its toll, you know."

"It's good to see you too, Tetrarch[7]. I am not sure that we have yet had the pleasure of your presence in the Temple."

"In a day or two, in a day or two. Now I see you are disturbing me with this interesting-looking prisoner. Who is he?"

The guard captain saluted and stepped forward.

"The procurator has written you this letter, sir."

"This gets more and more intriguing." He unrolled the papyrus and read it attentively. *"My goodness, so you are Iēsous, or if I'm not mistaken Yeshua Ish-Natzeret. Is that right, Kayafa?".*

"Yes, that is correct."

"Well, Yeshua," he said, continuing in fluent Aramaic. *"You have spent some time avoiding my company, and lo and behold, here you are, without my having to lift a finger. You might call it providential."*

Kayafa was finding it hard to contain his irritation and impatience. Yeshua stood imperturbably as if the occasion had nothing to do with him at all.

"Now that you are here, and apparently without any pressing matter to hand, I would like you to satisfy my curiosity on one or two points. I have been told that you were responsible for the healing of

the young son of one of my officials, and that from a considerable distance.[8] Tell me, Yeshua, how did you do it?"

Yeshua was silent.

"No answer? How vexing. Is it perhaps because you disapprove of my building my splendid new capital of Tiberias - and providing employment to hundreds of local people - over a disused graveyard?[9] Am I a sacrilegious person in your eyes?"

Again, no response.

"Perhaps you simply have no respect for me, eh? I'm just 'that fox'.[10] I warn you, Yeshua, foxes can bite."

Still no response.

"Or do you blame me for your kinsman Yochanan's death? I regret that almost as much as you do. My hand was forced."[11] Herod paused, and looked for some reaction in Yeshua's face, but it remained impassive.

Kayafa could stand it no more. *"Your honour, this man stands before you under the most serious charges of blasphemy and sedition. He showed as little respect for the Great Council as he does to your nobleness. In his pride and madness he claims to be Ha-Mashiach, the son of the Blessed One, the coming Judge. Action has to be taken, particularly as Yerushalyim is always in a volatile state during major festivals like Pesach."*

A priest added, *"Yes, your majesty,"* Kayafa winced again but Herod looked rather pleased. *"He doesn't want people to pay their taxes. And he's a magician!"*

Herod looked decidedly amused. *"Really! Well, let's look again at our friend Pilatus' letter. So you claim to be Ha-Maschiach, do you? Well, well. I fear that an ancient politician like me is hardly* competent to adjudicate such a claim. The Sanhedrin don't seem to be in favour, eh Kayafa?"

The High Priest bowed in silent assent.

"You have indeed been one of my subjects, though as far as I am concerned, a very invisible one. But Ha-Maschiach, as we are all well aware, hails from Beit-Lechem, the city of David. In fact just a dirty little village and very appropriately called a bakery.[12] Anyway, as such, you clearly are the responsibility of the Procurator of Y'hudah and Samaria, so I am sending you back to him." He beckoned a slave. "Go and find Tertius and tell him I want to send a letter, now."

A couple of minutes later the secretary arrived with papyrus, pen and ink and sat down on a stool. Herod started dictating.

"Herod Antipas, Tetrarch of Galilee and Peraea to his Excellency Pontius Pilatus, Procurator of Judaea and Samaria. Greeting. I thank the God of our fathers daily for your firm governance of the Province. And I specially thank you for sending me the interesting prisoner Iēsoun, and your courtesy in acknowledging my interest in those who live in the territory appointed for me. I was interested to meet him, but sadly he's like one of the mute swans on my ornamental lakes - all feathers and no voice. However, on learning of his claim to be the Xristos, I believe that he now comes under your jurisdiction. Part of the claim traditionally includes provenance from the town of Bethlehem, the city of David in the territory of Judah. I therefore return him to you with my compliments.

"I would also like to invite you, my dear Pilatus, for dinner in my palace here at the end of the present feast. We shall then be able to enjoy decent bread. We have for too long allowed a few local misunderstandings to cloud what should, I believe, be a harmonious working relationship. I wish you the best of health, and as much serenity as this city allows.

"The eighteenth year of Tiberius Caesar, the seventh day of Aprilios in the morning.

"Now we shouldn't allow our distinguished visitor to leave empty-handed. Ha-Maschiach needs a kingly robe, surely." He called a household slave.

"Go and find one of my old purple cloaks - not a good one mind - and we'll put it on this dumb prophet. And a bronze brooch to keep it in place, a cheap one. Go on!"

After a few minutes' delay, a faded purple cloak was brought in and fastened with a brooch at the shoulder.

"Off you go, your Majesty," Herod said grinning, and the priests and guards could not help grinning themselves. Yeshua was marched unresisting out of the Tetrarch's palace and across the piazza back to the governor's headquarters.

The Governor's Headquarters/Praetorium - again

The group arrived at the Praetorium entrance. One of the high priest's guards handed Herod's letter to a soldier on duty who took it inside to the governor. After a few minutes, the soldier came back out to the group and said that the procurator wanted to interrogate the prisoner privately. As he escorted Yeshua inside, Kayafa gritted his teeth in annoyance and frustration. He ordered one of the guards, *"Go and find the captain and get whoever is in the Market Square inside on the Palace Pavement as soon as possible. And remind him that one prisoner due for execution today is the Zealot Barabbas. He's popular. Tell the crowd to shout for him. After fifteen years, I think I know how our esteemed governor's mind works. We've got to get this thing done."*

In a business-like room in the headquarters, Yeshua stood in front of the governor, who was seated on a camp chair.

"First, Iēsou, do you understand Greek?"

Yeshua nodded.

"Well, in case you don't understand something, this soldier here is fluent in Aramaic. You say you are Xristos. What does that mean? Are you a Zealot? Do you murder my men? If you are the king, are you aiming to raise a rebellion against the divine Caesar, Herod and me? Why shouldn't I have you crucified?"

Silence.

"Are you this King of the Jews?"

At last Yeshua spoke, And in simple Greek.

"It's as you say."

"So you admit it. You are a rebel!"

"My kingdom is truth."

"What? What mumbo jumbo is this? Don't you realise I've got the power to set you free or to order your death by crucifixion?"

Yeshua looked almost with pity at the middle-aged Roman military officer in front of him.

"You can only do what you can. All your power is delegated. So the one who brought me here carries the greater responsibility."

"What! I'm going to put an end to this. Soldier, take the prisoner to the guard room. Have someone tell the high priest I'm going to make a public announcement from the balcony. We'll see whose writ runs here!"

Soldiers placed the governor's official chair and side table with refreshments and writing materials on the first floor balcony overlooking the Palace Pavement. By the time everything was ready, a large crowd of Jerusalem citizens had swarmed through the fortified entrance, up the steps and on to the mosaic-paved piazza. Kayafa and a large body of Temple aristocrats, Council members, priests and Torah-teachers had gathered on the side of the porch beneath the balcony, facing both the governor and the crowd.

Pontius Pilatus came out and stood at the front of the balcony. He addressed the crowd, numbering about two thousand, in Greek. A soldier next to him translated it into Aramaic for those whose Greek was scanty.

"Citizens,..." Pilatus bellowed in his best parade-ground manner. *"Today, the feast of Passover,... I wish to continue the benevolent practice... which I, with the support of the divine Caesar, have held for the last fifteen years .... Of releasing one condemned prisoner..."*

Cheers, with several chanting *"Bar-abbas, Bar-abbas, Bar-abbas..."*

"Today, I am giving you the choice.... There are two condemned men here.... Iēsous from Nazareth who claims to be the Xristos .... (some boos)*... and Iēsous Barabbas*[13]*...* (cheers, with Bar-abbas, Bar-abbas, Bar-abbas chanted). Kayafa allowed himself the first genuine smile of the day.

"So do you want me to release Iēsoun the Xriston, the king of the Jews or the terrorist Barabbas?"

The crowd's chanting grew ever louder. *"Bar-abbas! Bar-abbas! Bar-abbas!"*

Pilatus took a step back, shocked at this reaction. He motioned to the centurion near him. *"This crowd is quite unmanageable. We should get the men and clear the square."*

"Excellency, that's always risky, particularly as the high priest and many of the Sanhedrin are there. It would be like declaring war on Jerusalem. We've no idea where it could end up."

"I suppose you're right. It goes against the grain, though. I don't like to see the high priest crowing. Well, if it's got to be done, it's got to be done."

Pilatus stepped forward to the front of the balcony again and held up his hand for silence.

"In the name of the beneficent and divine Caesar, I here proclaim the pardoning and setting free of Iēsou ...." he paused dramatically as the crowd had its breath. *"Barabbas!"*

The crowd went wild, cheering and whooping, clapping each other on the back. Even the two lines of soldiers drawn up in the colonnades on either side of the piazza smiled. Pilatus smiled a little grimly. With the crowd in a good mood, there should be no trouble in sorting out this without extreme measures.

"As for Iēsous so-called Xristos, Basileus Iudaeorum ...my decision is that he should receive a Roman flogging..." He made an aside to the centurion next to. him, *"That should wake him up."*

The crowd responded in confusion, shouting *"Serve him right! Let him go! Kill him!"* Kayafa whispered to the council members near him and they started up a chant of *"Crucify"* which gradually spread through the crowd. *"Crucify! Crucify! Crucify him!"*

Pilate lost control for the first time, going red in the face. *"Why? What harm has he done? What's his crime?"*

The crowd's chanting got even louder. *"Crucify! Crucify! Crucify him!"*

The soldiers on either side felt the crowd was beginning to get out of control and started fingering their weapons nervously.

Kayafa waited for a lull in the shouting, then stepped forward right in front of the balcony. *"If you let this man go, who says he's a king, you're no friend of Caesar."* Pilatus stared down at Kayafa for a long moment, then addressed the crowd.

"This man Iēsous claims to be your king. If he isn't, who is your king?"

Led from the front by the priests and Temple aristocrats, the ensuing muttering coalesced into the rhythmic chant of *'Caesar, Caesar, Caesar!"*

Pilatus smiled grimly.

"That's something we've got out of it," he said to the centurion.

"Well done, sir," was the reply.

Pilatus announced in a ringing voice, *"The sentence is that Iēsous so-called Xristos, Basileos Iudaeorum, is to be flogged and crucified."* Then more quietly, *"Centurion, go and prepare the cross. Make arrangements for the normal security detail. I don't see any particular risk here."*

Pilatus went back inside, and the crowd went back to their Pesach celebrations.

Notes on 15th Nisan/Friday morning - trials in the Praetorium and Herod's Palace.

[1]Sources: Mark 15.1-15, Luke 23.1-25, John 18.28 - 19.16

[2]Where did the trial under Pontius Pilate take place? There are three contenders:

   a) The traditional site at the start of the Via Dolorosa, under the convent of the Sisters of Zion. The problem is that the pavement was constructed a hundred years later by the emperor Hadrian over an enormous system of water cisterns. So not there.

b) The governor, or procurator, may have based himself while in Jerusalem in the gigantic Antonia fortress. It would be appropriate for the Praetorium to be at the heart of the procurator's army. The problem is, where would Pilate address the crowd? They surely would not let a volatile mob inside the fortress? And outside, there was simply the Temple, and an unwalled and undeveloped space next to the Pools of Bethesda.

c) Herod the Great built a vast palace just south of what is now the Jaffa Gate. Ten years after his death, Caesar stripped Herod Archelaus of his kingship and presumably took over his royal palace. Later, half of it was given to Herod Antipas, ruler of Galilee and Peraea. The other half was a Roman army barracks and the governor's residence when he was in Jerusalem. The 'Pavement' on which the trial was heard was the central space between the two wings of the palace. The fortified entrance faced the City Market or 'agora' - a tailor-made space for public assemblies. This means that the transfer between the Praetorium and Herod's palace took only a few minutes.

d) Based on the model of first century Jerusalem in the Israel Museum I have assumed that the central piazza was where the trial of Jesus took place. It is referred to by two words. The Greek Lithostrōtos refers to the elaborate mosaic design of the pavement. The Aramaic 'Gabbatha' shows that to Jerusalem residents the key fact was that it was raised about fifteen feet above ground level.

[3]My characterisation of Pilate is taken from Brigadier-General Dyer of the 1919 Amritsar massacre. He never thought he had done wrong in having between 375 and 1,000 unarmed civilians shot in a public square with no means of escape. Jesus referred to the Roman governor when he mentions "the Galileans whose blood Pilate had mingled with their sacrifices". (Luke 13:1)

Nothing is known about Pilate's life before he was procurator or Governor of Judaea, but there are certain guesses we can make. I assume that he served ten years on the Rhine or Danube frontier as a senior military officer. He may early on have shown particular skill with the spear or javelin. He came from a wealthy family as he was a member of the equestrian order, just one rank below senator. Kinsmen may have actually sat in the Senate. After he was recalled in some disgrace in 36 AD, he may have retired to Amelia in Umbria, central Italy.

Less than eighty years before his birth, the Samnite tribe in south central Italy, to which he probably belonged, fought for independence from Rome but was defeated at the battle of the Colline Gate, 82 BCE. The Oscan language of the Samnites disappeared in the first century.

[4]'Xairé', pronounced 'chairay' with 'ch' as in the Scottish word 'loch'. It means 'Rejoice', and was the normal greeting. The conversation between Pilate and Caiaphas would have been conducted entirely in Greek.

[5]'Ieesoo' is exactly how Pilate would have pronounced the Greek vision of Yeshua, in Greek Iēsou(s). The Greek version has different case endings: Iēsous if he is the subject, Iēsou if addressed directly, Iēsoun if he is the object, Iēsou if something is happening to or from him.

[6]I have taken my characterisation from Robert Graves' book 'Claudius the God', p. 16-17, 51-52 (Penguin).

[7]On Herod the Great's death in 4 BCE, his territory was divided into four parts. Herod Antipas was given Galilee and Peraea (in ancient times called Gilead), with the title of Tetrarch, meaning ruler of a fourth. His wife Herodias resented the fact that he did not have the title of 'king'.

[8]John 4.46-54

[9]From Josephus 'Antiquities of the Jews', 93 CE

[10]Luke 13.32

[11]Mark 6.14-29

[12]Beit-Lechem means 'house of bread', i.e. bakery.

[13]An early version of Matthew in Syrian and Armenian of the fifth century gives the first name of Barabbas as Jesus, (Matthew 25.16). An unlikely detail which could well be true. Yeshua was a common name. No other early versions give him a first name. I use it here.

15th Nisan

First Day of Unleavened Bread[1]

Skull Hill

Golgotha/Skull Hill

The Central Courtyard of the Roman Barracks

Yeshua was led by two soldiers down the stairs to the paved central courtyard. It was almost always in shade because of the two-storey building on all four sides. At one side stood a free-standing pillar with iron manacles fixed to the stone, eight feet above the ground. Yeshua stood silent as they stripped him of the purple cloak, his own woollen cloak, his long-sleeved tunic and even his loin cloth. He allowed his hands to be locked in the manacles without a curse or a complaint. Then nothing, until the tramp of a hundred pairs of heavy-soled sandals echoed round the courtyard.[2] Orders were shouted by the centurion and a hundred soldiers stood in ranks along one wall.

The centurion barked *"Men, you've been called here to witness a historic achievement. The prisoner, who claims to be the Xristos, or the king of this god-forsaken province, has been captured without a drop of blood being spilt. The procurator has sentenced him to crucifixion, so now comes the first part of his penalty, forty lashes. Who's going to volunteer for the first eight?"* Hands shot up, but discipline ensured that no one shouted out. The centurion said, *"Right, we'll start with you, Marcellus. Rufus, Hermes, Timon, and you too Jonam. Fall out and line up next to Marcellus. Carry on."*

The leather thongs with bits of bone and metal tied to the ends whistled though the air and tore into the flesh of Yeshua's back.

Crack! Gasp
Crack! Gasp
Crack! Gasp
Crack! Gasp

Blood began trickling down Yeshua's body. His face was set, his teeth clenched.

Crack! Gasp
Crack! Gasp
Crack! Gasp
Crack! Gasp

"Well done, Marcellus. Neat work. Rufus, you take over."

Crack! Gasp
Crack! Gasp
Crack! Gasp
Crack! Gasp

Blood was starting to seep through the bruises on Yeshua's back.

Crack! Gasp
Crack! Gasp
Crack! Gasp
Crack! Gasp

"Good, Rufus. Hermes, your turn."

Crack! Gasp
Crack! Gasp
Crack! Gasp
Crack! Gasp

The flesh of Yeshua's back was now a series of bloody ribbons.

Crack! Gasp
Crack! Gasp
Crack! Gasp
Crack! Gasp

The centurion was not without feeling. He admired the stoic silence with which Yeshua bore the torture. *"Prisoner, you're over half way through. Timon, carry on."*

Crack! Gasp
Crack! Gasp
Crack! Gasp
Crack! Gasp

The whip was now tearing into the exposed muscles of the back and buttocks.

Crack! Gasp
Crack! Gasp
Crack! Gasp
Crack! Gasp

"Not bad, Timon. Jonam, you're the last."

Crack! Gasp
Crack! Gasp
Crack! Gasp
Crack! Gasp

A pool of blood was spreading over the paving stones. Yeshua's legs could barely support him.

Crack! Gasp
Crack! Gasp
Crack! Gasp
Crack! Gasp

"Right, that's it. Release his hands."

Yeshua clung to the pillar for support as he slowly straightened up. The soldiers watched in silence, they could recognise physical courage when they saw it. Yeshua took some deep breaths, then stood away from the pillar and faced the hundred. No one quite knew what to do next. Then one young soldier said, *"Hey centurion, he says he's a king, and we've got his royal robe here. Why not treat him like a king?"* A gale of laughter broke the tension. The centurion grinned, relieved at not falling for the mistake of getting sentimental.

"A good idea, soldier, bring it here."

The faded purple cloak was draped around Yeshua's shoulders, hiding his nakedness, with the bronze brooch keeping it in place.

"Centurion, can I go outside and find a branch or something to make a crown?"

"Go on and look sharp. We haven't got time to waste."

The soldier ran out of the barracks and reappeared in a couple of minutes with two thin spiky branches, which he twisted in a circle and pushed on to Yeshua's head.

"Wow! He's a real king!" laughed one soldier. *"Your majesty!"* cried another.

The centurion took charge before the cohort degenerated into a rabble.

"Now men, stand in line! If we're going to do this, let's do it properly. On the count of three, shout 'Hail king of the Jews!' One, two three."

"HAIL, KING OF THE JEWS!"
"And again."
"HAIL, KING OF THE JEWS!"
"And again."
"HAIL, KING OF THE JEWS!"

Some knelt in mock homage, some spat at him, one soldier braved the centurion's wrath and got a bulrush stem from a standing vase in a corner and slashed it across Yeshua's face.

"OK, men, that's enough. Settle down. Straight lines. Attention! You two, step forward, take that purple cloak off him and help him put his own clothes back on. Yes, you can leave his royal crown on for now. You've done well, men. An extra ration of wine for you all tonight."

All but the four soldiers on crucifixion duty left the courtyard looking pleased as punch.

The Road to Execution

Yeshua staggered out of the courtyard, supervised by the four soldiers, through the entrance hall and onto the main piazza. The morning sun shone brightly on the marble buildings. There he waited while other soldiers brought up two criminals due for crucifixion that day, along with the crossbeams to which their hands would be fastened. The two other condemned men had been scourged the evening before and so had had some time to mend.

A small group of priests had stayed behind while the high priest went to supervise the day's worship in the Temple. A decurion came out and gave each squad of four soldiers a wooden board on which the crime was written out. *"Robbery and murder"* read two of them. The third one read, *"Melech Y'hudahim - Rex Iudaeorum - ō Basileus tōn Ioudaiōn"*. The priests instantly stiffened and one of them went to the solider on duty in the porch.

"Officer, we have to see the governor urgently. He's making a serious mistake!"

"I'll relay the message, reverend, but I don't think he'll be happy."

Five minutes later, Pilatus appeared in the porch, visibly irritated.

"Now what is the matter, priests?"

"Your Excellency, it's an important matter. The titles which will hang over this Yeshua's head giving his crime, says he is the King of the Jews. That's not right! He's not our king! He <u>said</u> he was the king of the Jews. Not our king at all!"

"Priest, I'm not going to stand here chopping logic with you. What I've written stays written. That's it." Before they could think of a reply, he had stalked back into the Praetorium.

The twelve man squad loaded the heavy cross beams onto the shoulders of each of the prisoners, two of them fluently cursing Rome, the soldiers and their fate. All three prisoners were made to walk across the mosaic pavement, down the steps to the main gate and out to the street opposite the City Market. Yeshua staggered and almost fell going down the stone steps. A soldier put his hand out to steady the cross beam. They turned left onto Market Street where a crowd of the curious had gathered. They quickly recognised Yeshua, because he was the only one wearing a tunic and cloak, and the wreath of thorns was still on his head. Jeers and catcalls greeted Yeshua, and some rotten fruit, until the soldiers made a threatening move towards the crowd and stopped it. A couple of hundred yards further, the party came to the Hippichus Gate, which Yeshua had walked through freely only half a day before. Just before reaching it, the weight of the crossbeam proved too much for him, and Yeshua collapsed on the flagstones. One of the older soldiers scanned the pedestrians entering through the gate and seized on a young man wearing a merchant's cloak and with an African-type face.

"Here, you, carry this crossbeam."

"It's got nothing to do with me. I don't even live here."

"I don't care. You're going to do it, and we're going to have no delay. Just up to that hillock outside the gate. Right?"

The young man with a Berber complexion looked ready to explode with resentment, but then he looked at the prisoner, whose expression of total acceptance, whatever happened, took the wind out of his sails.

"All right, come on, let's have it. If it'll help you, mate. Not because of these pigs."

He loaded the crossbeam on his shoulders and Yeshua followed him, at last able to walk upright. They walked along the path which skirted the city wall until they were opposite a small rocky hill, with its half dozen wooden uprights ready today to become the instruments of agonising death for three men. Skull Hill.

Skull Hill[3]

As the party climbed the rocky knoll, three bugle calls were heard faintly from the Antonia, marking the start of the morning watch. As they reached the top, a couple of elderly women offered each of the prisoners a drink from a jug they had with them - wine mixed with myrrh to deaden the pain. The two robbers drank greedily. Yeshua took one drink, then turned his head away.

Each squad of four soldiers took their prisoner, stretched them out on the ground and hammered a heavy nail into each wrist-joint. The two robbers shrieked in agony. Yeshua clenched his jaw convulsively, but at each hammer blow prayed aloud.

Bang
"Abba forgive."

Bang
"Abba forgive."
Bang
"Abba forgive."
Bang
"Abba forgive."
Bang
"Abba forgive."
Bang
"Abba forgive. They don't know - what - they do."

The soldiers tied the wrists of each prisoner tightly to the beams, to avoid the nails tearing through the ligaments and letting the upper body fall free. The youngest soldier had carried a ladder and some rope. They raised each crossbeam six feet off the ground and let it fall into the iron bracket on one of the uprights. One prisoner screamed aloud as his shoulder dislocated. Then they hammered nails through the ankles. The robbers had one giant nail hammered through both ankles; Yeshua had each ankle hammered through with separate nails. There they hung, each breath an agony, on top of the pain of the nails, and the continuing pain of the scourging. Finally, a soldier climbed the ladder to hang on a nail above the heads of the dying men the 'titulus' describing their crime.

Pain.

Pain.

Pain.

The four soldiers responsible for Yeshua's execution squatted on the ground and inspected their booty - sandals, tunic, belt, cloak.

"Look at this tunic! All woven in one piece. Someone's labour of love. Must have taken a whole year!"

"All right , we can't tear it ,and one sandal's no use to anyone! Let's dice for them all. Highest of three rolls gets first choice." He threw two bone dice and the other three joined in.

Pain.

Pain.

Pain.

A crowd of onlookers stood on the path by the city wall, less than fifty yards from the gruesome sight. Some were only too happy to see Yeshua suffering there.

"Hey, prophet, you still going to destroy the Temple and rebuild it in three days?"

"You going to get off the cross and stop me trading in the Temple again? I don't think so!"

One of the soldiers stretched himself and looked carefully at the 'titulus'.

"King of the Jews, eh? Not very powerful now, are you?"

He laughed nastily.

Pain.

Pain.

Pain.

There was a stir in the crowd standing opposite the crosses. A group of a dozen priests and Torah-teachers arrived. They looked grimly pleased with what they saw.

"Look at the famous healer! Needs some healing himself now!"

"O great Maschiach, come down from the cross now! Turn the nails into water! King of Israel, show us your power so we can see and believe!"

After an hour they got bored and went back to the Temple for a bite of lunch.

Pain.

Pain.

Pain.

Darkness.

"'Ere, what' happening? Gone a bit dark. P'raps we should have brought some lanterns. Weird." The soldiers started to feel nervous, but were definitely not going to show their comrades that they were frit.

Pain.

Pain.

Pain.

Darkness.

A group of half a dozen women arrived on the path, keening a lament and sobbing uncontrollably. Yeshua raised his head and searched the group. He tried to say something. An elderly woman and a young man came as close as the soldiers would allow. With every breath an effort, Yeshua said, *"Mother - your son. Son - your mother."* The young man bowed his head in understanding, put his arm around the woman and led her away weeping.

Pain.

Pain.

Pain.

Darkness.

Yeshua made a supreme effort, raised himself on his tortured feet, took a deep breath and made the terrible cry,

"Elohi! Elohi! L'mah sh'vaktani?"[4]

"'Ere, sound like 'e's calling for Prophet Elijah."

"Well, you'd know, you're one of them."

"Maybe he's thirsty."

"Oh yeah, he'll be thirsty all right."

"Look, I'm going to give him some of our plonk. Anyone got a sponge? Ta. A stick or a javelin? That's great. 'Ere you are, mate."

"Nah, stop it, let's see if this Elijah fellow will come down and take him away."

"Go on, get away, I'll just give him a drink."

Yeshua's whole body suddenly stiffened, his face lifted up to the sky, as he gave a last shout.

"It's done!"

His body collapsed down again, his head dropped to his chest. His lips moved for a few moments and then ceased. His chest was still.

Dead.

163

Notes on 15th Nisan/Friday day

[1]Sources: Mark 15.16-37, Luke 23.26-46, John 19.16-30)

[2]Mark tells us in one translation that the whole cohort was brought to witness the scourging. That would have been five hundred soldiers commanded by five centurions. However, the actual Greek word is 'speira', which unlike Roman military words, is very unspecific. It could be a cohort. It could equally be a small squad like that sent to arrest Jesus in Gethsemane. I have guessed that it was all the men under the command of the centurion responsible for that day's executions, i.e. a hundred soldiers.

[3]The place where Jesus was crucified was called in Hebrew 'Golgotha', meaning 'Place of the Skull'.

[4]Hebrew for 'My God, my God, why have you forsaken me?" (Psalm 22.1)

16th Nisan

Second Day of Unleavened Bread

The High Priest's bedroom

In Caiaphas' bedroom

The master bedroom of the Palace of the High Priest Caiaphas[1]

Kayafa was finally able to relax. The bedroom was on the first floor, a comfortable square room with one window facing the central courtyard and a handsome red and gold Persian wool carpet on the tiled floor. Taking off his formal cloak, he had on his short-sleeved linen tunic and undershorts. His wife had a similar, though longer, tunic. They helped themselves to a goblet of sweet Pramnian[2] wine and sat down together on the fleece-covered couch.

"By the holy Temple, I'm glad today is over," said Kayafa.

"It's been so stressful for you, Yosef." His wife Drusilla touched his arm. *"Do tell me all the grisly details."*

"You know, everyone knows, what turmoil this Galilean so-called prophet has created in the Temple this week. We thought we'd just have to overlook it until all the pilgrims had gone home, another week of biting our tongues. Anyway last night - can you believe it! - just last night, one of his inner circle, someone we'd managed to turn, came to us informing us that this Yeshua was not in Beit-Anyah, safe among thousands of his fellow-Galileans, but right here in the city with just eleven companions. Unbelievably, he'd decided to eat Pesach with his fellow-conspirators right under our noses. It was a golden opportunity we couldn't pass up. But it needed some nifty footwork. Arresting him could have started a serious popular revolt.

We had to get it all done and dusted before these northern fanatics found out what was happening to their precious prophet."

"My dear, that sounds impossible! What did you do?"

"I knew the only way to settle his hash was to get the Romans involved. You remember I was absent from most of last night's dinner? I went along to Pilatus to get him on side. He was reasonably co-operative and agreed to let us have a squad of ten soldiers with their decurion to go along with our guards to make the arrest. Unfortunately, the house our Judaean informant took them to was empty, our bird had flown."

"Oh no! What happened then?"

"Well, now comes the really amusing part of the story. This Yeshua had fixed on a rendezvous place if any of the companions got separated, and there he was, waiting for our friend Y'hudah, quite unaware that he was bringing along twenty armed soldiers! What I'd have given to be there!"

"What a comedy!"

"Yes, but not for him. And actually, not for me. I had only a few hours to get everything fixed. I got your father to use delaying tactics, which he did with his usual consummate skill."

"He's great, my Dad"

"Indeed he is. But he didn't get very far with this Yeshua, so he sent him off down to us before anything was ready. Fortunately, we had an empty dungeon to store our Galilean prophet in. I had determined that the trial would be here and not in the Temple - far too many people around, and my hall is big enough for a small Council meeting. By first light I'd been able to summon a sufficient number of reliable council members for the trial and had got the guards here to round up some promising witnesses."

"So after all your preparations, did it go smoothly?"

"Not exactly. The witnesses were uniformly hopeless, and I was in danger of losing the support of some of the council members. But looking carefully at this Yeshua, I thought that there might still be a way. He seemed just the type to hang himself out of sheer pride. So I asked him, 'Are you Ha-Mashiach?'"

"No! That was a big risk! And did he say yes?"

"He did more than that. He used the sacred name of the Blessed One. Of course, the Council exploded. Condemned him to death."

"So was it all sorted then?"

"Not by a long way. When we took him to Pilatus, the procurator started being very officious, asking tricky questions and in the end sending him over to Herod Antipas."

"You've never been a patient man, Yosef, you must have been going out of your mind!"

"Rather. Especially as Herod didn't really want to be bothered and sent him back to Pilatus."

"So that started all over again?'

"In a way. Our friend Pontius took him inside and questioned him privately. But that gave us the opportunity to arrange a large, excitable and local Jerusalem crowd to see that we finally got shot of him. With a bit of encouragement, the crowd went wild asking for Yeshua's crucifixion, and Pilatus, never a man of principle, caved in. So by mid-morning our man was nailed up to a wooden crosspiece and died some hours later. And not a whiff of violence from his so-called supporters."

"What a relief. But I can see why you're so stressed. Shall I call my maid in to give you a nice back massage?"

"Perhaps in a while. But let me finish the story first."

"There's more?

"A little. I had to go to the Temple to officiate at the sacrifices. Mid-afternoon, we got the news of his death, and just then the great curtain separating the Holy Place from the Holy of Holies tore itself in two, from top to bottom!"

"No! How dreadful? Who could have done that?"

"It's a total mystery. No one knows. Maybe this Yeshua was actually a wizard who had learnt his spells in Egypt. Anyway, it shook us all. And then I heard that my namesake, Yosef Ramatayim[3] from the Council, had gone over my head, and had appealed directly to Pilatus to have the body given to him for burial. He should have been thrown in the lime pit with the other two low-lifes."

"I've never liked him. Too priggish by far."

"He is. One of those annoying bleeding hearts. Anyway, their dead prophet is now lying in a rock tomb at the foot of Skull Hill. No wonder it hadn't been used. No one wants to be buried there!"

"Well, dear, come to bed. You've certainly heard the last of this troublemaker."

Notes on 16th Nisan/Friday night

[1] Sources: Mark 15.38-47

[2] A popular and expensive Roman variety

[3] Joseph of Arimathea

18th Nisan

Fourth Day of Unleavened Bread

A letter from Salome to her husband[1]

Jewish tomb near Megiddo

From Shlomit, faithful wife, to my beloved husband Yitzchak, and to El'azar[2] and all the supporters of our Rabbi Yeshua in Efrayim.[3]

Shalom aleikhem in the name of Abba Elaha.[4]

I thank Elaha constantly for your love and faithfulness which are such a support to me and all who love our Rabbi. I pray that he may continue to keep you safe from all our enemies and that we will see each other again very soon.

I have so much news to write to you! You won't believe it!

You know how I witnessed that terrible terrible torture of our beloved rabbi. I was in a group with all the sisters who are staying with the household of El'azar, Marta and Miryam here in Beit-Anyah. It was the worst day of my life, of all our lives. Standing there so helpless while he hung there in awful agony. It made me even feel pity for the two wretches being crucified with him. The soldiers seemed to show him some respect at the end. And then seeing the nails wrenched out of his feet and wrists and his poor broken body laid out on the ground. The soldiers refused to let us get near; it was heart-breaking. Imagine our astonishment when we saw a Council member in an expensive embroidered cloak coming with four slaves carrying linen, wrapping his body in it and taking it away to an unused tomb at the foot of the hill. They closed it properly, so at least his poor dead body was safe from his enemies. I don't know how that man managed to get permission to do that, but I bless him for it.

Of course by then you and El'azar were well on your way to Efrayim. I guess you got there by sunset. None of us knew if El'azar might not be the next on the list, and it was important for you to go with him. As women we were probably safe. I thank Abba Elaha every hour for the brave hospitality of the people of that town. They are a true city of refuge for us, as they were for our rabbi only two months ago.

What a dreadful Shabbat that was. We didn't dare to go out, we hardly ate, we sat and lamented, taking it in turns to keen for him. We could hear the other pilgrims making their way to the Temple, but we stayed inside. I went across to Shim'on's house to check that the brothers were safe. They were, apart for Shim'on Kefa. No one knew where he was, and they were very worried about him. And of course the traitor didn't dare show his face. So no longer the Twelve - they were now the Ten. The front gates of both our houses were securely locked and bolted. We were all on tenterhooks, jumping at the smallest sound, but nothing bad happened.

After dark, Miryam of Magdala, Miryam - Ya'akov's mother, Yochana and I went to buy spices to anoint our rabbi's body in the morning. We avoided the Temple, going down the Kidron to the Fountain Gate and then to Spice Street near the racing stadium. It looked pretty with the lanterns hanging over the stalls with their colourful array of spices, but it was a sad and difficult task. The first merchant we went to was quite chatty and sympathetic when we told him it was for a burial. But when we told him who it was for he got angry, spat on the ground and told us to take our custom elsewhere. I didn't realise how much these Judaeans hated our rabbi. The next one wasn't so chatty and sold us the spices without asking any questions. The moonlight made the walk back easy. Still, we were relieved to get back safely to Marta and Miryam's home in Beit-Anyah.

Miryam of Magdala woke us up really early, all four of us who
had been out with her the night before. After washing our hands,
we wrapped ourselves in our cloaks and went out. There was
just the faintest hint of pale sky in the east. We walked down the
Mount of Olives, and past the Roman fortress, ignoring the wolf
whistles from the soldiers guarding the main gate of the Antonia.
We skirted the city wall till we came to the spot where our rabbi
had died. As we got closer, we realised that the stone blocking
the grave entrance would still be in place. We didn't know if the
combined effort of the four of us would be enough to shift it.
Perhaps a stranger might help us. We did not want any of the
Twelve to get involved - they had almost been arrested two days
ago. But when we got there, there wasn't one grave that was shut!
We knew it wasn't a popular place because of where it was.[5] It
gave me the cold shivers to be right at the spot where our rabbi
had suffered that cursed death. But Miryam of Magdala strode
straight up to one of the black square openings, and then shrieked!
We ran up to her and stood rooted to the spot. In the early morning
light we could just see a young man dressed in a white tunic
sitting on the body slab on the right-hand side inside the grave.
We were about to turn tail and flee when he announced, clear as
clear, *"Don't be shocked. You're looking for Yeshua Ish-Natzaret,
the crucified one. He has been raised; he isn't here. Look, here is the
place they put him."*

We were speechless. We didn't know whether to run or stay.

*"Go and tell his trainees, and go and tell Shim'on Kefa, that he is
going ahead of you. He's going to the Galil. You'll see him again, just
as he said."*

Our nerve broke and we ran out of there as if our lives depended
on it. When we got half way along the city wall, Miryam of
Magdala stopped.

"That man - whoever he was - told us to tell Shim'on Kefa."

"But we don't know where he is," wailed Yochana.

"I have an idea," she replied. *"You go back and tell the rest of the brothers. I'm going into the city. I think I know where he might be."*

We found out later that she had guessed that Shim'on Kefa had taken refuge in the house of Yochanan of Yerushalayim, along with Miryam, the mother of Yeshua, and she was right. Shim'on and Yochanan both ran to the grave and found the linen grave clothes in an empty tomb. Miryam of Magdala followed them walking and stayed alone at the grave. And listen to this!

Yeshua, our rabbi, met her there! Alive! She raced back to us and by mid-morning all of us, men and women, had heard her story. We just didn't know what to believe. Was she just being hysterical, or could it possible be true?

Then Shim'on Kefa turned up at the door, knocking loudly. He was like the old Shim'on, excitable, enthusiastic, strong. He said that Yeshua had met him too!

Next morning, we had more news. The previous night, the Eleven were roused by Cleopas and his wife who had just hurried back in the dark from Amma'us. It was not far off the middle of the night when they got here. They gasped out their news that they had just spent two hours with Yeshua and almost had a meal with him! Not surprisingly, everyone started talking at once, so much so that for a little time they didn't realise that Yeshua was right there standing among them! Absolutely unbelievable!

T'oma had been out staying with family and when he got back in the morning, said roundly that he didn't believe a word of it.

So that's our amazing news! The faces of our brothers now shine with a new hope and joy. It's wonderful but hard to know, what now? I guess that if anyone is going to credit it, it's El'azar, because he's been there. We're going to stay here for a few more days, at least to the end of the feast. What happens then only Abba Elaha and our rabbi Yeshua know.

All the brothers and sisters here send their greetings, especially Marta and Miryam.

I too send my greetings, Timon of the household, who wrote this letter.[6]

May Abba Elaha's steadfast love and faithfulness be with you.

Notes on 18th Nisan/Monday – Letter from Salome

[1]Sources: Mark 15.40 -16.8, Luke 24, John 20.1-25, 1 Corinthians 15.3-8

[2]Shlomit is is the Hebrew version of Salome. We do not know if she was married. I have presumed she was, for the sake of the book. She could of course have written it to someone else like her sister.

El'azar is called Lazarus in the gospels. John 12 recounts how Jesus raised him from death, and that thereafter he was next on the Jerusalem priests' execution list.

[3]John 11.54 says that Jesus and his disciples withdrew to Ephraim in the wilderness after the raising of Lazarus. It was too risky for him in Jerusalem without the protection of a large pilgrim crowd. Ephraim had its name changed to Taybeh by Salah-ed-Din around 1200 in recognition of their hospitality. It is a wholly Christian village, very proud of their having provided a refuge for Jesus. I have guessed that it is where some of the disciples fled to after the crucifixion.

[4]Peace/well-being be to you in the name of Father God.

[5]Over half a dozen rock-cut tombs are in the vicinity of the tomb venerated as that of Jesus in the Church of the Holy Sepulchre. Archaeologists have recently found the original limestone burial bed beneath the traditional tomb.

[6]Women did not receive a formal education in the ancient world, so Salome would have dictated the letter to a literate slave of the household. Another servant would have walked to Ephraim/Taybeh to deliver it.

Seven weeks later...

6th Sivan

The Feast of Shavu'ot[1]

Report from the Captain of the Temple to the High Priest Kayafa

Lower City and the river Kidron

El'ichud Bar-Nachum, Captain of the Temple

To Yosef Bar-Kayafa High Priest

Greetings.

I thank Adonai Elohim for the good governance which your wisdom and diligence have given to the people of Yerushalayim and Yisrael for so many years. In your high priesthood the people have experienced both peace and prosperity. Long may it continue.

I beg to report a disturbance in the city which took place this morning, in the very shadow of the Temple. A crowd of several thousand pilgrims gathered in the square below the Huldah Gates.[2] They were addressed by a leading member of the group that followed the condemned blasphemer Yeshua Ish-Natzeret. He is known as Shim'on Kefa. He asserted that Yeshua's death was a fulfilment of prophecies in the Readings, and that in his case the Holy One, blessed be he, had brought forward the general resurrection, which these enthusiasts, like the Hasidim, believe in. He claimed that this miracle, which has not been witnessed by anyone outside the immediate circle of his followers, proves that he is Ha-Mashiach. I am sorry to say that the crowd, consisting mostly of Jews from the Dispersion, were taken in by this story. They were then persuaded to have themselves baptised in the name of Yeshua Ha-Mashiach, and several thousand were shepherded through the Lower City to the Valley Gate, from where the twelve members of Yeshua's inner circle took them and baptised them in the river Kidron.[3] It lasted the entire day. It was a scene of religious fanaticism we have not seen since the days of Yochanan the baptiser.

There are, in my view, only two saving graces. The first is that the Romans probably remain unaware of the event, because it happened on the opposite side of the Temple from the Antonia. But you may wish to inform the governor out of courtesy. The other is that most of the crowd involved seem to have been pilgrims from the Dispersion, and so after the feast, the number of local sympathisers will in all probability be small.

In the meantime, I have detailed two of my men to work out of uniform and keep an eye on this new populist religious movement. It is strange that whereas after Yochanan the baptiser's death his movement dwindled, after the death of Yeshua Ish-Natzeret his movement seems to be growing.

I wish you health and shalom.

The seventh day of Sivan, Feast of Shavu'ot, mid-afternoon.

Notes on 6th Sivan Feast of Shavu'ot/Pentecost Sunday

[1]Shavuot is Hebrew for 'weeks' and means that it follows Passover a week of weeks later, i.e. forty nine days. So it was called by Greek-speaking Jews 'fifty', or Pentecost. It marked the wheat harvest, as Passover marked the barley harvest. It was one of the three pilgrimage feasts of the Jewish year, the third being Sukkot which marked the end of the fruit harvest. In Shavuot, farmers would bring their first fruits to the Temple and make the declaration set out in Deuteronomy 26.1-11. It was held on just one day in Israel and over two days in the Diaspora.

[2]Working on the basis of the model of 1st century Jerusalem in the Israel Museum, it seems that the only available open space for a very large

crowd would be south of the Temple below the Huldah Gates. These had an enormous flight of steps leading up to the Temple, an ideal spot from which to address a crowd.

[3]The Acts of the Apostles tells us that three thousand were baptised that day. Assuming that all the twelve apostles took part, that would equate to each man baptising 250 people over the ensuing eight hours. That is thirty baptisms an hour by each of the twelve apostles, with no break for lunch. That is one baptism per apostle every two minutes. The only place that could have happened was in the fast-flowing river Kidron. Even allowing for some exaggeration of numbers, it was clearly a massive public event. No wonder the Temple Captain was worried.

Explanations

The Story of the Book

The Eagle Comic

This book was started about 65 years ago. I was then a boy at boarding school and every week would read the Eagle comic. It had brilliant cartoons strips like Dan Dare and Sergeant Luck of the Legion. And on the back page there were the life stories of various famous Christians like David Livingstone. Once, they did the life of St Mark, the gospel writer. I still remember how the finding of the Upper Room was portrayed, and the first attempt to arrest Jesus. It took the Bible narratives as a basis and created intelligible scenarios of what could have happened in practice. Some of the dialogue I use in the book is a direct lift from the Eagle, remembered after all those years.

The Man Born to be King

In my teens I discovered the radio plays of Dorothy Sayers *The Man Born to Be King* – a series of 12 radio plays going through the whole life of Christ. Again, I saw how imagination linked to historical sources can bring the story to life. It is the same with all historical novels, from *I Claudius* by Robert Graves to the trilogy on Thomas Cromwell by Hilary Mantel. The result is a 3-D portrait which brings the characters to life. Only loosely can they be called works of fiction because the history is carefully researched and transformed by the writer's imagination to create characters that live.

Discovering Mark

At Merton College, Oxford I studied history. It was a time when my Christian faith came alive for me. The two ways of thought coalesced in my conviction that the Gospel of Mark is the nearest we have to a first-hand account of the ministry of Jesus. It includes details which are absent from the other gospels and which are there simply because they happened. For instance, when Jesus calmed the storm at sea (Mark 4.35-41), only Mark tells us that 'other boats were with him.' And crucially, when Jesus swept the traders out of the Temple, only Mark tells us that 'he would not allow anyone to carry anything through the Temple.' That means he had to seize control of the gates by outnumbering the temple guards. It was not a demonstration. It was an occupation!

Parish Life

After a number of years in personnel management, I eventually read theology at Durham University and became a vicar, first in Kingston-upon-Thames and then for 21 years in Hackbridge and Beddington Corner, between Croydon and Sutton. We had parish communion each Sunday, so every Sunday I preached on the gospel reading. I got to know the gospels quite well. I found Matthew difficult, because I think that, compared with the other gospels, he is unreliable. I explain my reasons for this in 'Examining the Gospels'. Also, every Holy Week I would choose daily readings which accompanied Jesus through the actual events of those days as recorded in Mark. This is different from the official readings which all concentrate on Jesus' suffering and death on Good Friday. I liked to get a sense of Jesus' actual experiences day by day.

Writing Books

I retired in 2015 and started writing books. I discovered that Chris Day, who played the organ for weddings in Hackbridge, was a publisher. He has been my partner publisher and mentor ever since. I remember the first question he asked me when we discussed my being an author was, *"What are the next two books you will write?"* My first book was *'Bible in Brief'*- a six-month workbook giving an overview of the Bible, allied to a website of the same name. Since then, I have published blogs, sometimes weekly, sometimes monthly, under the overall title, 'Making Sense of the Bible', plus four other books, the details of which can found at the end of this book.

The Germ of an Idea
Since the summer of 2019 I have been working on *Has the Church Got a Future – Being Credible in the Post-Modern World*. I paused this when coronavirus hit, because I thought we could be entering a very different world. In the summer of 2020, I thought I would write a book for Holy Week, following Jesus day by day as I used to when I was vicar of Hackbridge. I saw it as accompanying a series of bible readings, with the title *'Making Sense of Holy Week'*. However, I think God had other ideas.

Writing a novel
On Monday 21st September, at about 3.00 in the afternoon, my wife Linda and I were driving along the A303 back from visiting her parents in Plymouth. Linda was driving and I was turning over some ideas for my book on Holy Week. Suddenly, the phrase popped into my mind, 'it was hot in the Jordan valley.' I realised immediately that this was not the start of a devotional or intellectual book. It was the start of a novel. I had never attempted a novel before, but was instantly excited about the idea.

On Thursday 24th, I went out to The Courtfield pub at 9.00 to make a start of writing this book on my Mac laptop, aided by a pint of Guinness. While there, I had another idea, whether from Guinness or God you can choose, namely the title of the book: *'The Troublemaker'*. Just over two months later, I sent it off to my editor, my nephew's wife Jo, who is both kind and efficient. And now you have it in your hands (or on Kindle).

The Challenge of Fiction
It has been a most exciting couple of months. Writing a historical novel is much more exacting than writing a commentary or devotional.

First. I had to be precise in both timings and geographical locations. For instance, Mark tells us that Jesus arrived late at the Temple on Palm Sunday. Why did he arrive late? Because he had just walked uphill for 18 miles from Jericho. What was the walk like? Was water available? (No). Where had he spent the night before?

Second. Where there is conflict between the different gospels, I had to choose. When did Jesus clear the traders from the Temple? At the start of his ministry (John 2.13-25) or at the end (Mark 11.15-19)? I followed Mark. Was Jesus anointed at Bethany two days before Passover (Mark) or six days before Passover (John)? I compromised on four days. Did Mary/ the woman anoint his head or his feet? My answer – his feet. At the end of each section, I explain in the notes the reasons for my choices.

Third. There is the need for invention to fill in the gaps. The day before Jesus walked to Jerusalem was the Sabbath. He would naturally have gone to synagogue and been asked to speak. What did he say? I lifted something appropriate from an earlier point in his teaching ministry. Jesus had arranged a secret sign to keep the place of the Last Supper safe. How did he arrange this? For this I invented a short episode in the Temple on Wednesday afternoon, which also becomes the trigger to Judas' act of betrayal. It probably did not happen like that, but *something* like that happened. And, of course, the conversation between Caiaphas and his wife in their bedroom is fiction, but is a useful device to bring in incidents like the torn curtain in the Temple which I could not otherwise cover.

Fourth. There was the need for re-invention of Jesus' words. The whole aim of the book is to bring Jesus to life, to extract him from the stained glass of church tradition, to make him our contemporary. So, I have taken his words as a starting point and re-interpreted them in a way in which he might be speaking in 2021.

For instance, when James and John ask for the best places in the coming kingdom, Jesus says, *"You do not know what you are asking. Are you able to drink the cup that I drink, or be baptised with the baptism that I am baptised with?'* (Mark 10.38). In my version he says, *"You haven't a clue what you're asking. Can you pass the test I will be taking? Or can you sign up for the same struggle?"*

I believe that this gives the sense of what Jesus meant.

Sources

When I retired, I gave away half my books. Writing in lockdown meant that I had no access to theological libraries. However, I had kept the basics: Greek New Testament, Greek lexicon, concordance, commentaries, the Jewish New Testament, the Atlas of the Bible and my Jewish Prayer Book. I got *'The Temple'* by Edersheim (1875) and *'The Testimony of the Beloved Disciple'* by Richard Baukham from Amazon. And invaluable, consulted every day, was the internet, particularly Wikipedia. It answered innumerable questions such as: What is the temperature of Jericho in March? When is sunrise in Jerusalem in early April? Who was Pontius Pilate? What is nard?

Thanks

When I had finished the main book, I discovered that my nephew's wife did editing as a sideline. Enormous thanks to Jo Roland for the excellent job she did on a very complex text, as well to my friend David Goymour. To my publisher and mentor, Chris Day. To my friend Nat Gillett who created the fabulous cover. To the book designer Clare Clarke and to my illustrator Daniel Gould who I got to know five years ago while driving home from a karate club dinner. To Tony Gelston, who was my theology tutor at Durham, for his guidance on my use of Aramaic. And to my wife for her unfailing and astute support throughout. Any mistakes in the book are mine and mine alone.

Andy Roland

Examining the Gospels

There are five crucial questions when considering the reliability of any historical document, including the Bible.

1   Who wrote it?
2   How near to the events was it written?
3   Does the author intend to be truthful?
4   Is he actually truthful or does he let his prejudices get in the way?
5   What do other sources say?

The Case of Mark

1   Who wrote it?
There is no reason to doubt that Mark wrote the gospel. He was only a bit player in the gospel story. His mother's house was a meeting place for the early church (Acts 12.12). He may be the young man in Gethsemane "wearing nothing but a linen cloth; they caught hold of him, but he left the linen cloth and ran away naked." (Mark 14.51)

2   When was it written?
Since I believe that Luke wrote his Gospel and Acts during Paul's arrest and imprisonment in 62 AD, and he quotes large chunks of Mark's gospel, Mark must have been written at least before 60. Most New Testament scholars say that it was written before 70. I think it was written about 55, about 20 years after Jesus' death.

Compared with Luke and Matthew, Mark tells the stories in greater detail, indicating access to a first-hand witness.

3   Did he mean to be truthful?

Mark writes as a person of faith, but there is every sign that he means to record faithfully the stories he had heard. Clement of Alexandria (150 - 215) says that Mark wrote down what Peter had preached and wrote it down for the Christian community in Rome.

4   Did he succeed in being truthful?
a) A first-hand source

Mark has details which indicate a first-hand source. E.g. when Jesus calmed a storm on the Sea of Galilee, only Mark notes that 'other boats were with them'. When Jesus threw the traders out of the Temple, only Mark tells us that this was the day after Jesus' arrival: 'Jesus entered Jerusalem and went into the Temple; and when he had looked around at everything, as it was already late, he went out to Bethany with the twelve.' (Mark 11.11) And only Mark relates, that next day, in addition to throwing the traders out, Jesus 'would not allow anyone to carry anything through the Temple.' (Mark 11.16)

b) Awkward facts

Mark does not gloss over awkward facts. When a young man asks, "Good Teacher, what must I do to inherit eternal life?" Jesus gives the uncomfortable answer, "Why do you call me good? No one is good but God alone." (Mark 10.17, 18). Above all, Mark unflinchingly records Jesus' cry, at the end, "My God, my God, why have you forsaken me?" This does not come in Luke or John.

c) Problems

The long passage in Mark 13 which describes the future destruction of Jerusalem and the second coming of Christ is, I believe, an amalgamation of different sayings said at different times. And one was put in later because it breaks up the passage it is inserted in: *'And the good news must first be proclaimed to all nations.'* (13.10) - an extremely popular text with preachers. But not, I think, original.

5   What do other sources say?
The gospels of Matthew and Luke fit well into Mark's framework. They do provide more of Jesus' teaching, but all his healing acts come from Mark. Paul in 1 Corinthians tells of Jesus' words at the Last Supper, and they are virtually identical to the words in Mark. (Mark 14.22-23, 1 Corinthians 11.23-15).

Conclusion:
Can we trust Mark? I would say yes.

The Case of Luke

1   Who wrote it?
Luke never met Jesus. He was a Gentile doctor, a Christian, and a companion of Paul.

2   When was it written?
When Luke wrote his gospel depends entirely on when he wrote the Acts of the Apostles, because that is Volume 2 of a two-volume work. I believe that Acts was completed while Paul was in prison in Rome, before he suffered martyrdom i.e. around 62 AD. My reasons for believing this are:

a) The book tails off with Paul under house arrest in Rome. It is quite an anti-climax to end the book with. He was not even bringing the gospel to Rome, because there were already Christians there to greet Paul when he arrived. (Acts 28.15)

b) The first 19 chapters cover a period of 25 years. The last eight chapters cover about four years, simply, I think, because Luke was there. They are a first-hand account.

c) A major thrust of the argument of Acts is that this new Christian group should be treated as a *'religio licita'* – a legal religion. He quotes numerous decisions by Roman officials to show that they did not think it was illegal. Once Nero in 65 AD had declared the Christian sect illegal, being a Christian became a crime punishable by death for the next 250 years, and the arguments of Acts were largely redundant.

d) Luke says he had 'investigated everything carefully'. (Luke 1.3) When might he have done his investigations? My guess is during the two years that Paul was in prison in Caesarea so Luke could visit people in Palestine, i.e. around 59-61 AD. (Acts 24.24-27) That's within living memory.

3   Did he mean to be truthful?:

"I too decided, after having investigated everything carefully from the very first, to write an orderly account for you, most excellent Theophilus..." (Luke 1.2) So Luke did mean to be truthful. Did he succeed?

4   Did he succeed in being truthful?

Luke tells us his gospel is a composite account. That raises two questions:
1   Is he faithful to his sources? and
2   Are his sources reliable?

1 What were his sources?

a) Mark's gospel. He is faithful to Mark; so we can assume he is faithful to his other sources. For instance, when in Mark Jesus disconcertingly responds to an enthusiastic young man by asking, *"Why do you call me good?"*, Luke reports the same words. By contrast, Matthew changes it (to protect Jesus' reputation?) to *"Why do you ask me about what is good?"*

b) Q stands for the German 'Quelle' meaning 'source'. For over a hundred years Biblical scholars have accepted that there was a common source behind the sayings that Matthew and

Luke have in common. In fact, I think that there were several sources:

Q1 Written documents, e.g. sayings of John the Baptist. Pretty reliable.

Q2 Sayings handed down by word of mouth, similar but with some differences; e.g the Lord's prayer in Luke has 38 words (in English); Matthew has 50.

Each case has to be decided on its own merits.

c) L - Luke's special material. This includes some of the best loved parables, like the Good Samaritan, the Prodigal Son, the Pharisee and the Tax Collector. And very human stories of Martha and Mary, Zacchaeus and the penitent thief. There is no reason to doubt their authenticity. He has his own tradition of Jesus' arrest and crucifixion, which he probably wrote down before he discovered Mark. In particular, he mentions the hearing under Herod Antipas and has different quotations from Jesus on the cross.

5   What do other sources say?
Apart from Mark, there are no other sources against which to check Luke's account, but his use of Mark is a good litmus test which Luke passes well.

In summary:
A reliable secondary account, with some unique parables and stories.

The Case of Matthew

1   Who wrote it?

Despite the early tradition of the church which put Matthew at the start of the New Testament, I think we can safely say that the apostle Matthew had nothing to do with the making of the gospel which bears his name. There is nothing in it that indicates a first-hand account. Instead, it is a compilation of a whole series of sources: Mark's gospel, some written documents and some oral traditions, possibly Palestinian in origin. So what can we know about the writer?

a) The writer was a Jewish Christian. The very first verse of the gospel: *'Jesus Christ, son of David, son of Abraham'* could only have been written by a Jew.

b) He wrote in smooth, polished Greek. Perhaps he lived in the Diaspora, i.e. outside Palestine.

c) He had an organised mind. Jesus' teachings are collected into five distinct blocs, according to subject matter: chapters 5-7 the Sermon on the Mount; 10 the mission; 13 parables of the kingdom; 18 the church; and 23-25 judgement and the end of the age.

Perhaps 13.52 is a self-portrait: *'Every scribe who has been trained for the kingdom of heaven is like the master of a household who brings out of his treasure what is new and what is old.'*.

2   When was it written?

We don't know. It was certainly written before 100 AD because Bishop Ignatius of Antioch quotes it in his letters written about 106-107 AD. Verses such as Matthew 22.7 indicate that it was written after the destruction of Jerusalem in 70.

3 Did he intend to be truthful?

I think the answer is yes and no. He was careful to reproduce stories and sayings from his sources, but if there was a problem with something, he editorialised.

4 Did he succeed in being truthful?

I am sorry to say that the writer of Matthew does let his opinions and prejudices get in the way. In four ways. He is sometimes 'churchy'. He enjoys people being punished. He enjoys a good miraculous event, even when they may not have happened. And he does gild the lily in stressing Jesus' divinity.

a) Churchiness

Some sayings in Matthew are better suited to the early church than to Jesus, the radical rabbi of Galilee. The beatitudes we see in Luke (*'Blessed are you who are poor, woe to you who are rich...'*) are spiritualised – though still challenging – in Matthew (*'Blessed are the poor in spirit'*). When it comes to forgiveness, Matthew gives us rules for dealing with a church member who sins (Matthew 18.15-18); and Jesus' uncompromising teaching about divorce and remarriage - (in no circumstances is it God's will) is given a get-out clause for adultery (Matthew 19.9)

b) Punishment

Matthew often adds material which stresses the idea of God punishing people. Both Matthew and Luke tell the parable of the great banquet to which the invited guests refuse to come and the rich man (king in Matthew) invite the riff-raff off the streets. But Matthew has an extra bit of the story. *'The king noticed a man who was not wearing a wedding garment... he told the attendants, "Bind him hand and foot, and throw him outside, into the darkness, where there will be weeping and gnashing of teeth"'*. (Matthew 22.11-14) The phrase 'weeping and gnashing of teeth' occurs six times in Matthew, once in Luke and never in Mark or John or Paul. I think they have been added by Matthew, or by his church.

c) Adding a miracle

There are six episodes recorded in Matthew alone (excluding the infancy narratives which I regard as a special case).

- Peter walking on the water (14.28-32) Is it a sermon illustration that got out of hand?
- Pilate's wife's dream (27.19) How did Matthew know?
- Judas' suicide (27.3-10) Possible compared with Luke's parallel story in Acts 1.18-19.
- Earthquake 1 (27.51-53), when Jesus died and several dead people rose from their graves. No hint of this in the other gospels. Because it didn't happen?
- The Guards (27.62-66, 28.11-15) Why only in Matthew? Was it a later tradition?
- Earthquake 2 (28.2) Sounds like a scene directed by Cecil B de Mille, of 'The Ten Commandments' fame. Contrast it with the sober account in Mark and John.

d) Gilding the lily

Matthew frequently changes words to reflect an attitude of worship of Jesus. E.g. when Jesus walked on water, his disciples *'were utterly astounded.'* (Mark 6.51) Matthew writes, *'Those in the boat worshipped him, saying "Truly, you are the Son of God."'* How we react to that depends on our personality, i.e. do we look for historical truth or theological truth. I favour the former.

5   What do other sources say?

The only other accounts are in Paul's First Letter to the Corinthians, written in 56 AD. Paul describes the Last Supper (11.25-26) and the Resurrection (15.3-8). He mentions Jesus' appearing to Peter, to over 500 followers, to James, as well as to himself.

Conclusion:

If we only had Matthew's gospel, we would still have the basic facts and teachings of Jesus. But on its own, his gospel tends to blunt the radical strangeness of Jesus' ministry in favour of a dogmatic theology of Jesus as the Son of God. And he introduces events and miracles which have no other support and I believe did not happen.

The Case of John

I used to say, in answer to whether the gospels were reliable: Mark – yes, Luke – largely yes, Matthew – no, John – God knows! The gospel of John is an amazing book but is it history or theology or art?

I was one week away from putting out a blog on John's gospel, when I happened to read 'Testimony of the Beloved Disciple' by Richard Baukham, and had all my ideas turned on their head. Here is what I think now.

1   Who wrote it?

For the last 1900 years it was believed that the writer was John, son of Zebedee, a fisherman from the Lake of Galilee. But how could he write such a strange book when all the action takes place in Jerusalem?

Richard Baukham's argument is that there was another disciple called John but living in Jerusalem. John, or Yohanan, was a common name. It is possible that both Johns ended up together in Ephesus at the turn of the century.

If there was a Jerusalem disciple called John, that explains why, apart from chapter 6, only 22 verses of the first 20 chapters take place in Galilee. It also explains why all the geographical descriptions about Jerusalem pre-70 are accurate.

If John of Jerusalem was the disciple whom Jesus loved, it is worth noting that the only other disciple we are told Jesus loved was also from near Jerusalem, Lazarus from Bethany. Jesus clearly had a whole network of secret disciples in Jerusalem about whom the Twelve know little or nothing. (Mark 11.1-3, 14.3, 14.12-15, 15.43)

2 When was it written?

It was certainly written in the first century. The earliest papyrus fragment of the New Testament comes from John 18 and is dated by the writing style to about 125 AD. You can see it in the Rylands Library in Manchester. Beyond that, it is a matter of conjecture. There are myriad theories of how it might relate to the other three gospels. My personal view is that it makes better sense if written before the destruction of the Temple in 70 AD, but no one knows. The tradition is that both Johns lived to a very great age in Ephesus.

3 Did he intend to be truthful?

Up to a point. Baukham points out that ancient biographies were very different from biographies today. It was important to get the geography and time right, and you had to have had first-hand experience. But the actual speeches and dialogues were created by the author, who knew the person, but in the writer's own style. It was a rhetorical culture, in which the spoken word was pre-eminent. For example, all the writings of Plato are dialogues with Socrates, who mentored him. But how much is Socrates and how much is Plato remains an insoluble problem.

I think John intended to be truthful in the same way that I do in this book – to give a living portrait of Jesus, to be accurate in all the incidents, and then to create speeches and dialogues which give the sense of what was said.

4 Did he succeed in being truthful?

This has to be taken on a case-by-case basis:

John 2.13-22

John places the cleansing of the Temple at the start of Jesus' ministry. I follow Mark in placing it at the end. But I do include the challenge about Jesus' right to do this, because it was a key accusation at his trial before Caiaphas.

John 11

The raising of Lazarus from death. The big question for preachers is why the other gospels do not include such a striking miracle as part of Holy Week. The answer is simple. It happened a month or so earlier. Jesus then left and went to the town of Ephraim, now Taybeh, in the West Bank. Because without the protection of large pilgrim crowds, it was too dangerous for him to stay in Jerusalem. Only one puzzle: why did he return to Jerusalem via Jericho?

John 12.20-33

The Greeks seeking Jesus. No reason to doubt it. And a very useful incident for me to have as a scene in the Temple on Thursday morning.

John 13

Washing the disciples' feet. Not mentioned in the other gospels. There maybe a hint in Luke 22.27: "I am among you as one who serves." A question remains at what point in the Passover meal it would have happened.

John 14-17

I have not included these long and inspiring talks. Was John present at the Last Supper? As the host? As an honoured guest?

John 18.12-23

The hearing before Annas makes perfect sense, geographically and chronologically. If John was known to the High Priest (Annas or Caiaphas) he is a valuable witness (John18.15). How would a Galilean fisherman know them?

John 19.26-27

"Woman, behold your son ... and he took her into his own home." I.e. a safe house in Jerusalem, Not a village in Galilee five days walk away!

John 20.1-18

My guess is that Simon Peter took refuge in the same safe house as Jesus' mother did. That would explain why it was just he and the beloved disciple who ran to the tomb, and how Mary Magdalene could come to be there on her own.

Did he succeed in being truthful?

I would say, as far as the events are concerned, yes. The dialogues need to be taken with some discernment.

What do other sources say?

The only other sources are the first three gospels. I take Mark as my primary source, aided by Luke, with John supplying some other material. For instance, when Jesus was arrested, John makes it clear that there were both Roman and Temple troops there.

Jesus is mentioned in passing by later Roman writers, always unfavourably, and in two mediaeval manuscripts of the Jewish historian Josephus, but they add nothing of substance.

Conclusion:

John writes in a way to help us encounter Jesus in the present: *'Now Jesus did many other signs in the presence of his disciples, which are not written in this book. But these are written so that you may come to believe that Jesus is the Messiah, the Son of God, and that through believing you may have life in his name.'* (John 20.30-31)

Jesus in Context

William Blake's famous poem/song/hymn 'Jerusalem' has the lines:

> *And did those feet in ancient times*
> *Walk upon England's mountains green?*
> *And was the holy Lamb of God*
> *In England's pleasant pastures seen?*

The answer, of course, is no. Jesus never left Palestine, as far as we know, and he lived in a very different culture and civilisation from ours. This article will look at the three major dimensions of difference between our world and that of Jesus: Languages and Names; History and Politics; Religion and Division.

Languages and Names

'Yeshua' in Aramaic script

Languages

India under the British Raj was a continent of 238 million people and 22 languages. The lingua franca which was used for business and government was English. Palestine in Jesus' day was similar. There were countless 'barbarian' languages spoken through the Roman Empire, but the lingua franca was Greek. So the New Testament was written in Greek. And two Galilean fishermen could give one of their sons each a Greek name, i.e. Andrew and Philip.

However, for the native population of Palestine there were two languages to contend with. The normal everyday one was Aramaic, the common language for much the Middle East. It was closely related to Hebrew, but by about 400 BCE, Jews no longer understood their ancient language and they had to have the relevant passages from the Torah explained in Aramaic (Nehemiah 8.8). We have some examples of Jesus' actual Aramaic words: Abba = Father; talitha = little girl; kumi = get up; ephphatha = be opened. (Mark 5.41, 7.34)

But Hebrew was still an important language, because it was the language of religion and law. By 200 BCE most Jews living outside Palestine could no longer understand Hebrew, so their Scriptures were translated into Greek. However, anyone who took their religion seriously would have known enough Hebrew to study the Torah. In his last cry of agony on the cross Jesus quotes the first verse of Psalm 22, but he quotes it in Hebrew, 'Elohi, Elohi' and not in Aramaic, 'Eloha, Eloha'.

Names

The first move in stepping into Jesus' culture is to get his name right. The problem is that the New Testament was not written in Jesus' native language, Aramaic, it was written in Greek. And the problems with Greek were:

1   it had no way of reproducing the sound 'sh' - so they used 's' instead;
2   the sound 'Y' was written as 'I" which could be 'y' or 'i' and got transformed into English as 'J';
3   it had elaborate case endings.

So Jesus' Aramaic name was Yeshua and would be the same in each of the following sentences . But when his name was transformed into its Greek version, it would appear as follows:

> Iēsous blessed the children.
> O Iēsou bless me!
> The priest blessed Iēsoun
> Please give me the blessing of Iēsou
> The priest gave a blessing to Iēsou or Iēsoi

These variations are reflected in the way Pilate, or Pilatus, speaks. Yeshua is simpler!

The same issues arise with the names of other disciples, such as Simon Peter, which should read Shim'on Kefa (Kefa being Aramaic for Rock, Latin Petros). He could be called Shimeon. Paul always called him simply Kefa or Cephas.

The name Ya'akov is particularly confusing. In Latin the letter 'I' was used for I, J and Y. So 'Ya'akov got changed to Iakobos, later on to Iakomos, then to Giacomo or Iago in Italian and finally to the

English name James. Jake is our nearest equivalent to the original.

With Judas, once you take away the Greek final letter 's', the name clearly comes from Y'hudah, or Judah.

Jews up to the 18th century would have had their own name plus their father's name. So Judas son of Simon becomes Y'hudah Bar-Shim'on, using the Aramaic word for 'son'. In the book I only give the Hebrew for son 'ben' to particularly learned individuals. It means exactly the same. Son of man could be Ben-Adam or Bar-Enosh without any difference in meaning.

Latin names were more complicated. Romans usually had three names, a casual, personal name like Caius, but we don't know what Pilate's casual name was; a family or clan name like Pontius; and a personal official name such as Pilatus (the javelin-thrower). Not unlike names in India. So Gandhi's proper name was Mohandas Karamchand Gandhi: Gandhi the family surname; Karamchand from his father and Mohandas his personal name. His well-known name Mahatma was actually a title meaning 'Great Soul" and was given to him by popular acclaim when he was in his mid-forties. In the same way Jesus was given the title of Rabbi or even Rabban by his followers, though he probably had not studied in any recognised religious school.

Places

Throughout the book, I have used Hebrew names for places in order to embed the story in its proper Jewish culture. When I have visited Jerusalem in the past, I used to feel mildly offended when Israelis called it Yerushalayim. Of course, they were right and I was wrong! Simple things like that can affect our attitudes. There are only two places where I use the Western spelling., namely the river Jordan rather than Yarden, and Samaria instead of Shomron.

Dates and Times

The Hebrew names of the months have been used, which is an advantage because Passover always occurs on 14th Nisan. This did need some adjustment by the religious authorities however. The Hebrew calendar has twelve months a year, but they are lunar months, starting at the first sighting of a crescent moon. This makes them eleven days a year too short. As a result, every two or three years (actually seven times every nineteen years) an extra month is added at the year's end.

A major difference between Jewish and European times is that for Jews the day starts at sunset. For Europeans it starts at midnight technically, but in practice, with the advent of artificial light, when we get up the next morning. So when we are told that after the crucifixion the disciples rested on the sabbath, that began at sunset. When the sabbath ended the women disciples could go in the dark and buy oils and spices from the city merchants.

One final difference. No one had watches or clocks or i-phones. Time was divided into sections of the day or night - the third hour, the sixth hour etc. This was judged by the position of the sun in the sky. So there are no precise indications of time in the book. At one point I changed "an hour later" to "some time later". Perhaps a more relaxing way to live?

All the names used in the book can be found in the thematic glossary at the back of the book.

History and Politics

*Drachma of Tiberius, b.42 BC,
Roman emperor 14-37 AD*

To understand the complex situation of Jews at the time of Jesus, we need to think of the history which gave a framework to their lives in society. Or rather, the histories, plural. There was Ancient History, Recent History and Contemporary History.

Ancient History

Jews looked back to Abraham as their father in faith, a wealthy nomad who moved from what is now Iraq to the land of Canaan/ present day Israel. That would be as long ago for us as the departure of the Roman legions in the face of attacks by the barbarian Angles and Saxons. The crucial event in the story of the Hebrews and their formation as a people was their escape from Egypt, their deliverance from the army of Pharaoh and their adoption of a whole series of laws and religious regulations.

After their occupation of Canaan and the ensuing genocide, the twelve tribes were united under the great king David and his son Solomon around 1000 BCE - the same gap in time for Jesus as King Canute and the battle of Hastings (1066) would be for us. Then followed the split of the kingdom into two unequal parts - the wealthy one, Israel, in the north whose capital became Samaria, and the poorer one in the south, Judaea, centred on Jerusalem. Both were destroyed by the rival empires of Assyria and Babylon in 722 BCE and 597 BCE respectively. Longer ago than the defeat of the Spanish Armada is to us. Fifty years after this disaster the Jews were allowed to return and begin rebuilding Jerusalem and the temple, but it was hard going.

This ancient history defined the very existence of the Jewish people. Still today, every year Jewish families gather at Passover to recall the escape from Egypt . This ancient history is who they are.

Jesus shared this heritage, handed down in what he called the 'the Law and the Prophets'. He quoted from it frequently both in his disputes with the Pharisees and Sadducees and at the very end of his life, while dying on the cross.

Recent History

More recent history is that of the previous four hundred years which defined the boundaries of Jewish life. The First Book of Maccabees, written about 150 years before the birth of Jesus starts its account with Alexander the Great, who died in 323 BCE.

'After Alexander son of Philip, the Macedonian, who came from the land of Kittim, had defeated King Darius of the Persians and the Medes, he succeeded him as king. (He had previously become king of Greece.) He fought many battles, conquered strongholds, and put to death the kings of the earth... After this he fell sick and perceived that he was dying. So he summoned his most honoured officers, who had been brought up with him from youth, and divided his kingdom among them... Then his officers began to rule, each in his own place. They all put on crowns after his death, and so did their descendants after them for many years; and they caused many evils on the earth'.

(1 Maccabees 1.1,2,8,9)

Alexander's conquests spread Greek civilisation and the Greek language around the whole of the Middle East. For instance, Jerusalem in Jesus' day had an amphitheatre, a racing stadium and an 'agora' or city market. Just five miles from Jesus' home village of Nazareth where people mostly lived in caves, was the large and prosperous Greek-style city of Sepphoris.

A major consequence of the Greek take-over was the expansion of the Jewish 'diaspora' community all around the Mediterranean. Alexandria in Egypt was a particularly vibrant Jewish centre. The Pharaoh Ptolemy I (305 - 282 BCE) brought 120,000 Jews from Palestine to Egypt and more followed. By Jesus' time there may have been as many Jews living in and around Alexandria as in Palestine. They were allocated two of the five sections of the city and they were the only people group in Egypt to have their own independent political community. Philo of Alexandria (20 BCE - 50 CE) gives theJewish population as one million. Libya, Cyprus, Crete, Babylon and Rome were other major centres. It was in Alexandria that the Hebrew scriptures were translated into Greek. Several books of the Apocrypha probably originated there too.

In 175 BCE the Seleucid king, i.e. the Greek king in charge of the former Persian empire, tried to make Jerusalem an ordinary Greek city, with worship of the normal gods of the ancient world, disregarding all the commandments of the Hebrew Scriptures. The result was a fiery revolt under the Maccabee brothers against both the Seleucid armies and against those Jews who were happy to adopt the Greek lifestyle. In 166 BCE they captured and rededicated the temple, an event which is still celebrated in the feast of Hanukah each December. The Maccabee high priests were called Hasmoneans and they ruled for over a hundred years. About 100 BCE they destroyed the Samaritan temple on Mount Gezirim (according to Josephus, c. 93 AD) - not a good way to foster positive community relations. And in 104 BCE they conquered Galilee, converting its people to Judaism. Had it not been for the Maccabees, would Jesus have been Jewish?

In 63 BCE the Roman general Pompey, Julius Caesar's main rival, brought Judaea under Roman control through client kings. This is just like the British Raj in India where some territories were ruled by semi-independent local kings, such as Kashmir and Hyderabad. Herod, a semi-Jewish southerner seized power about 33 years before the birth of Jesus and undertook massive building projects, including the coastal city of Caesarea, numerous palaces including Jerusalem, Jericho and Masada, and of course the Temple. When he was dying, he imprisoned the elders of all his towns in the Jerusalem amphitheatre with orders that when he did die they should all be killed. This was so there should be some public mourning on his death. Fortunately his orders were not carried out.

Jesus lived within the conflicting cross-currents of Greek civilisation and his Jewish heritage. He received from this history a faith that was grounded on 'the Law and the Prophets', the impressive Temple festivals, and a sense of oppression by Roman taxation and military occupation as well as by the wealthy Jewish religious establishment. Although he was courteous to Gentiles he met, he was clear that his primary mission was to call the community of Israel to a new and living faith in the God who had revealed himself in their ancient history. Matthew adds to Mark's account of the healing of the Syro-Phoenician's daughter (Mark 7.24-30) the saying *"I was sent only to the lost sheep of the house of Israel."* (Matthew 15.24). That seems to me an accurate 'mission statement'. It was the experience of the Holy Spirit followed by persecution by the Jewish authorities which thrust the early Christian community out into the Gentile world.

Contemporary History

Just after the birth of Jesus, king Herod died and his son Archelaus became ruler of Judaea and Samaria. He was such a terrible ruler that Caesar sacked him. From then on Judaea and Samaria were governed by a Roman procurator. This put Judaea firmly into the Mediterranean-wide 'Common Market' of the Roman empire, with no borders from Calais to Cairo. The Roman procurator in Jesus' day was Pontius Pilate who governed from 26 to 36 AD. He clearly thought being in charge meant having a firm hand, carrying out several massacres of the people to maintain order. Jesus spoke of the 'Galileans whose blood Pilate had mingled with their sacrifices.' (Luke 13.1)

The procurator took it upon himself to appoint the high priest, and if he did not like him, to sack him. Annas was high priest from 6 to 15 AD. He was followed by three high priests who were appointed and dismissed in the space of four years. Then Caiaphas, Annas' son-in-law, was appointed and he stayed in power for eighteen years. His seat of authority was the enormous Temple built by Herod - one of the wonders of the ancient world.

Galilee, along with Peraea on the other side of the Jordan, was ruled for forty two years by another son of Herod, Herod Antipas, who admired Greek civilisation but was sensitive to Jewish religious feelings. He founded the city of Tiberias on the Lake of Galilee which is still there today. It was this Herod Antipas who was responsible for the arrest and subsequent execution of John the Baptist. When Jesus was told that Herod wanted to arrest him, he called him 'that fox' (Luke 13.32).

Jesus refused to get involved in the power politics of the time. I once sat on the Mount of Beatitudes overlooking the Lake of `Galilee and read through the first ten chapters of Mark's gospel. What was striking is that you could trace almost all his journeys from that vantage point. It was clear that he deliberately avoided the centres of power such as Tiberias, just a few miles away, or Sepphoris just five miles from his home in Nazareth. What he did was to attack the rich, especially the wealthy priestly elites in Jerusalem.

Politics

Neither the Roman Empire nor the Jewish community were democratic. Rome was a military autocracy. The Roman emperors were so anxious over any sign of local co-operatives that c.110 the emperor Trajan even forbade the formation of a local volunteer fire brigade in Bithynia (north Turkey), because such organisations could lead to trouble. The Empire did give Jews the special

223

privilege of allowing their contributions to the empire-wide tax for the state religion of Jupiter/Zeus to be used to support the Temple in Jerusalem. That is, until the Jerusalem Temple itself was destroyed in the Jewish revolt in 70 AD.

The main functions of the political system were keeping order, including patrolling roads in search of bandits, organising the law courts, and building large public works such as roads and aqueducts, all of which had to be paid for. This is where Pilate got into trouble. He used money from the Temple treasury to build a much-needed aqueduct for Jerusalem. When a protest crowd collected in front of the Praetorium, Pilate's headquarters, he sent soldiers into the crowd in disguise and, at a signal, they started beating the protesters with clubs, causing many deaths. The only appeal against misrule, was to the Roman emperor himself.

In Judaea local government was in the hands of an oligarchy of powerful priestly families based in Jerusalem known as the Sanhedrin or Assembly. This had been in existence for a century. It regulated the calendar, appointed judges to local courts, redeemed land from gentile ownership, applied the rules governing the sabbatical year (every seventh year the ground should lie fallow), determined divorce conditions, and made judgements on the status of Hellenistic/Greek-speaking cities within the land of Israel. Of course, being both the leaders of the establishment and being the judges meant that they never had to worry about an adverse verdict.

The ordinary citizen had no way of changing anything, except through mob action, which is why the authorities were so often heavy-handed. This included the priestly families of the Sanhedrin known as the Sadducees.

'Woe unto me because of the house of Boethus
Woe unto me because of their clubs! ...
Woe unto me because of the house of Ishmael ben Phiabi,
Woe unto me because of their fists.
For they are high priests,
And their sons are treasurers,
And their sons-in-law are law officers,
And their slaves beat the folk with sticks.'

(Babylonian Talmud, Pesahim 57b)

There was an opposition movement, called kana'im in Hebrew and Zelotes in Greek, in English Zealots. Josephus says it was founded in 6 CE by a Galilean, Judas of Gamala, in protest at the Roman census that was carried out then. They were violently opposed to the Roman occupation, to foreign, i.e. Greek, traders, and to the rich and powerful Sadducees. They may have been linked to the terrorist "dagger-men" or sicarii/siquaryim who used short daggers to attack Roman soldiers and Roman sympathisers alike. One of Jesus' twelve disciples, Simon or Shim'on, may have been one of them in the past. They were the leaders in the revolt against Rome in 66 AD which brought about the total destruction of Jerusalem and the Temple.

Despite some attempts by modern scholars to portray Jesus as a zealot and to claim that he was crucified as a political rebel, there is nothing I can see in the gospels to support that theory. Jesus' agenda was very different, a call to renew the very heart of Judaism.

Religion and Division

Jerusalem from the road leading to Bethany. Coloured lithograph by
Louis Haghe after David Roberts, 1842.
Attribution 4.0 International (CC BY 4.0)

Religion in the Roman Empire

The Roman Empire was full of religions. There were the traditional gods, worshipped under a variety of names, with major temples as the focus of their worship. Paul's preaching about Jesus nearly generated a major riot in the city of Ephesus, with a mob shouting *"Great is Artemis of the Ephesians"* for over two hours.

Then there were the philosophers who taught people to live a worthwhile life and who pursued an intellectual approach to religion. Luke records the encounter of St Paul with some philosophers in Athens.

'When Paul came to Athens, he was deeply distressed to see that the city was full of idols. So he argued in the synagogue with the Jews and the devout persons, and also in the market-place every day with those who happened to be there. Also some Epicurean and Stoic philosophers debated with him. Some said, *"What does this babbler want to say?"* Others said, *"He seems to be a proclaimer of foreign divinities."*... Now all the Athenians and the foreigners living there would spend their time in nothing but telling or hearing something new.' (Acts 17.16-18, 21)

Then there were the mystery religions. These were imported from the countries of the east like Persia and Egypt and they spread all over the empire. To join you had to undergo an a secret initiation ceremony. The (literally) underground rituals of Mithras were particularly popular with the military. The worshippers of the Egyptian goddess Isis believed she encompassed all the feminine divine powers in the world.

Religion pervaded all aspects of life. So the meat sold in the meat market would have been from animals sacrificed in pagan temples – a major problem for the first mixed Gentile and Jewish Christian communities. (See 1 Corinthians 8)

The Jewish Religion

The Law/Torah
'Hear O Israel the Lord our God the Lord is One.' (Deuteronomy 6.5) 'You shall not make for yourself an idol ...You shall not bow down to them or worship them.' (Exodus 20.4-5)

'Remember the sabbath day, and keep it holy. For six days you shall labour and do all your work. But the seventh day is a sabbath to the Lord your God; you shall not do any work.' (Exodus 20.8-10)

'You shall not eat flesh with its life, that is, its blood.' (Genesis 9.4)

A few sentences were enough to set Jews apart from all other ancient cultures.

This meant that for observant Jews, the Hellenistic cities of Palestine such as Tiberius, Sepphoris and Caesarea would have been regarded as morally impure, because of their inevitable idolatrous worship and questionable sexual practices. Also, Jew and Gentile could not eat together. As Peter said to God after receiving a disturbing dream, *"I have never eaten anything that is profane or unclean."* And when Peter entered the house of the Roman centurion Cornelius, he said, *"'You yourselves know that it is unlawful for a Jew to associate with or to visit a Gentile; but God has shown me that I should not call anyone profane or unclean."* (Acts 10.14, 28)

Typically, Jesus did not feel bound by the purity rules. When the centurion in Capernaum sent Jewish elders to ask Jesus to heal his servant, Jesus set off straightaway to his house. It was the centurion who wanted to keep Jesus from breaching the Jewish rules. *"Lord, do not trouble yourself, for I am not worthy to have you come under my roof; therefore I did not presume to come to you."* (Acts 7.6-7)

The way of life laid down in 'the Law and the Prophets', as Jesus called the Jewish scriptures, was very attractive to many thinking citizens of the empire. Every synagogue had its fringe of 'God-fearers', those who followed the basic precepts of Judaism but without converting and taking on the whole law. An example is the Roman centurion Cornelius: 'He was a devout man who feared God with all his household; he gave alms generously to the people and prayed constantly to God.' (Acts 10.2)

Jesus frequently got into trouble with the religious establishment for healing people on the sabbath. Here is a typical instance:

'Jesus was teaching in one of the synagogues on the sabbath. And just then there appeared a woman with a spirit that had crippled her for eighteen years. She was bent over and was quite unable to stand up straight. When Jesus saw her, he called her over and said, *"Woman, you are set free from your ailment."* When he laid his hands on her, immediately she stood up straight and began praising God. But the leader of the synagogue, indignant because Jesus had cured on the sabbath, said to the crowd, *"There are six days on which work ought to be done; come on those days and be cured, and not on the sabbath day."* But the Lord answered him and said, *"You hypocrites! Does not each of you on the sabbath untie his ox or his donkey from the manger, and lead it away to give it water? And ought not this woman, a daughter of Abraham whom Satan bound for eighteen long years, be set free from this bondage on the sabbath day?"* When he said this, all his opponents were put to shame; and the entire crowd was rejoicing at all the wonderful things that he was doing.' (Luke 13.10-17)

The Synagogue and the Sabbath

Most towns and villages in Judaea and Galilee would have had a synagogue, usually comprising a prayer hall and a study room with a mikveh (ritual bath house) nearby. There were meetings for worship every sabbath and it was Jesus' invariable practice to attend and to speak. He had already started his teaching and healing ministry when he returned to his home village.

'When he came to Nazareth, where he had been brought up, he went to the synagogue on the sabbath day, as was his custom. He stood up to read, and the scroll of the prophet Isaiah was given to him. He unrolled the scroll and found the place where it was written:

'The Spirit of the Lord is upon me,
    because he has anointed me
    to bring good news to the poor...'

And he rolled up the scroll, gave it back to the attendant, and sat down. The eyes of all in the synagogue were fixed on him. Then he began to say to them, *"Today this scripture has been fulfilled in your hearing."'* (Luke 4.16-18, 20-21)

Synagogue worship was the bread and butter of the Jewish faith wherever there were Jews. Even in a Roman colony like Philippi (which followed strict Roman laws and so had no synagogue), Luke tells us 'on the sabbath day we went outside the gate by the river, where we supposed there was a place of prayer; and we sat down and spoke to the women who had gathered there.' (Acts 16.13)

The Temple and the Festivals

King Solomon built the first temple at Jerusalem, completing it in 957 BCE. It was destroyed by the Babylonians 360 years later. A smaller temple was built about 516 BCE. King Herod did a major rebuild between 20 and 10 BCE, expanding it enormously. After the destruction in 70, the rabbis said wistfully, 'whoever has never seen the temple of Herod has never seen a beautiful building.'

The Temple came into its own during the three great annual pilgrimage feasts, as set out in the Torah: Passover in early April, Shavuot or Pentecost in mid-May and Sukkot or Tabernacles in October. When Jesus was 12 years old his parents took him for the first time to Passover in Jerusalem (and lost him on the way back). E P Sanders suggests that there could be 300,000 to 400,000 pilgrims at Passover. Josephus (93 AD) calculated almost 3 million on the basis of the fact that one Passover 256,500 lambs were sacrificed.

All the gospels record Jesus' final appearance at the Temple at Passover. John portrays him as a loyal Jew, being at two Passovers, as well as his attending one unnamed festival (John 5.1), plus the feast of Sukkot or Tabernacles in October (John 7), and the winter festival of Dedication or Hanukkah (John 10.22-39).

Division

In Dorothy Sayers' detective novel'Gaudy Night' Lord Peter Wimsey remarks, *"the first thing a principle does, if it really is a principle, is to kill somebody"*.

The root of the word 'religion' means binding together. Sadly, all too often it becomes a source not of unity but of division. That was most certainly the case in Jesus' world. The first main division was between Jews and Samaritans.

Samaritans

The Samaritans identified themselves as the descendants of the northern kingdom of Israel, surviving after the destruction of Samaria by the Assyrians in 722 BCE. The actual religious practices of the Jews and Samaritans were similar: the same Torah (the first five books of our Old Testament), the same Sabbath observance, the same food laws, much the same purity laws, the same requirement of circumcision. The primary distinction between them was the question of God's chosen place for his temple – Jerusalem or Mount Gezirim. Relations were not improved when around 100 BCE the Jews under the Hasmoneans destroyed the Gezirim Temple.

One incident which shows the hostility was when Jesus' messengers 'entered a village of the Samaritans to make ready for him; but they did not receive him, because his face was set towards Jerusalem.' (Luke 9.52-53).

In another instance Jesus, returning from Jerusalem, rested outside the town of Sychar.

'A Samaritan woman came to draw water, and Jesus said to her, *"Give me a drink."* (His disciples had gone to the city to buy food.) The Samaritan woman said to him, *"How is it that you, a Jew, ask a drink of me, a woman of Samaria?"* (Jews do not share things in common with Samaritans).' (John 4.7-9)

Clearly Jesus would have nothing to do with this prejudice, as can be seen by his parable of the Good Samaritan (Luke 10.25-37).

Jewish Divisions

Writing in 75, just after the destruction of the Temple, Josephus describes the four main Jewish groups. We need to bear in mind that he was writing for a non-Jewish audience.

Sadducees

The Sadducees were at the top of the tree. They were the priestly aristocracy based on the Temple in Jerusalem. They were traditionalists in terms of the Torah, compromisers in terms of the Roman occupation, and unpleasant in general. Josephus tells us that 'they hold that God is incapable of either committing sin or seeing it; that men are free to choose between good and evil; and that each must decide which he will follow... The permanence of the soul, punishments in Hades and rewards they deny utterly.'

Pharisees

In his 'Antiquities of the Jews' (93), Josephus reckons the number of Pharisees as around 6,000. They emerged around 160 BCE from the scribes and sages who carried on the Jewish tradition after the destruction of the First Temple. Their ideal was for the whole nation to keep the rules of ritual purity normally limited to priests. They believed that if all Israel did that for one day, the Messiah would come.

By the time of Jesus, Pharisees were in most towns and villages, an elite Jewish group, devoted to keeping all the 613 rules of the written and oral Torahs. 'Agrippa the Prince asked Rabbi Yohanan ben Zakkai, *"How many Torahs does he give you from heaven."* He answered him, *"Two, one in writing and one to be transmitted orally."'* (Neusner, 'A Life of Rabban Yohanan ben Zakkai' p. 171)

Yohanan ben Zakkai founded a Jewish academy in Jabneh after the fall of Jerusalem which enabled the Jewish faith to survive. It was told of him 'that he did not neglect a single Scripture or Mishnah, Gemara (interpretation of Mishnah), halakah (law), agada (legend), supplement (branch of oral law), or the subtleties of Scripture, or the subtleties of the scribes, or any of the sages' rules of interpretation..." (Neusner p.26).

There were many discussions about points of the Law, which were debated in a sort of central committee. Around Jesus' birth the two leading Pharisee schools were the stricter school of Shammai (you could only divorce your wife for adultery) and the more lenient school of Hillel (you could divorce your wife for burning the toast). The latter summarised the whole of the Torah as follows: *"What is hateful to you, do not do to your fellow: this is the whole Torah; the rest is the explanation; go and learn".*

After the destruction of the Temple, it was the Pharisees who created rabbinic Judaism, as we know it today.

Jesus had many disputes with Pharisees, mainly over what they saw as his lax attitude to keeping the Law.

Essenes

We know much about the Essenes because of the discovery of the writings of their community at Qumran on the shores of the Dead Sea, the Dead Sea Scrolls. Josephus, who had lived among them, describes them like this:

'The Essenes profess a severer discipline; they are Jews by birth and are peculiarly attached to each other... Their rule is that novices admitted to the sect must surrender their property to the order (at the end of their first year there, author's note), so that among them all neither humiliating poverty nor excessive wealth is ever seen,... but as with brothers their entire property belongs to them all....

'They possess no one city but everywhere have large colonies. (After the morning work) they ... wash all over in cold water... They then go into the refectory in a state of ritual cleanliness as if it were a holy temple and sit down in silence.... The priest says the grace before meat... It is indeed their unshakeable conviction that bodies are corruptible and the material composing them impermanent, whereas souls remain immortal for ever.'

A quote from their 'Community Rule': 'Prayer rightly offered shall be as an acceptable fragrance of righteousness, and perfection of way as a delectable free will sacrifice." (IX.5).

They were implacably opposed to the Sadducees in the Temple, whose leader they called 'the wicked priest'.

Did John the Baptist come from an Essene community? Luke tells us he 'lived in the desert until he appeared publicly to Israel.' What was Jesus' relationship with them? They are not mentioned once in the whole of the New Testament. Does that imply ignorance or agreement?

Zealots

Another group implacably opposed to the Sadducees, as well as the Romans, were the Zealots. They were created through Judas of Galilee's failed rebellion against Rome in 6 AD (Acts 5.37). Josephus said in 'Antiquities', 'they agree in all other things with the Pharisaic notions; but they have an inviolable attachment to liberty, and say that God is to be their only Ruler and Lord.' They were at the forefront of the disastrous rebellion against Rome in 66 AD. During the siege of Jerusalem in 68, the Zealots fought and defeated the provisional government, killing 12,000 people. Two years later, the city was sacked by the Romans and the Temple destroyed. The last Zealots died at the siege of Masada in 73.

Despite one of his 12 disciples being described as 'Zelotes', there is no indication that Jesus saw the Zealots' position as anything but a bringer of disaster.

Galilean Charismatics

Geza Vermes, a Jewish New Testament scholar, has argued in 'Jesus the Jew' (1976) that there was a strain of charismatic Judaism within Pharisaism, centred particularly in Galilee. Their rabbis' reliance on personal inspiration over against the written and oral tradition caused Yohanan be Zakkai to exclaim, *"Galilee, Galilee, you hate the Torah! Your end will be to be besieged!"* (Neusner p. 29)

Here are two stories:

Rabbi Yohanan had only one student from Galilee, Hanina ben Dosa. When the son of Gamaliel (the most senior Pharisee) was ill, he sent two disciples to Hanina to ask his prayers on the boy's behalf. When Hanina saw them, he went to the upper chamber of his house and prayed for mercy. When he came down he said to the disciples, *"Go, for the fever has left him."* *"And are you a prophet?"* they asked. *"I am neither a prophet nor a son of a prophet, but I am accustomed to discern thus: if the prayer is fluent*

*in my mouth, I know that it is accepted, and if not, I know that it is
rejected."* (Neusner p. 29-30)

A century earlier, another miracle worker, probably from Galilee, is
depicted:

Once they said to Honi the Circle-drawer: *"'Pray that it may rain."* ...
He prayed and it did not rain. Then what did he do? He drew a circle
and stood in it and said before God: *"Lord of the world, thy children
have turned to me because I am as a son of the house before thee.
I swear by thy great name that I will not move hence until thou be
merciful towards thy children."* It then began to drizzle. *"I have not
asked for this,"* he said, *"but for rain to fill cisterns, pits and rock-
cavities."* There came a cloudburst. *"I have not asked for this, but for
a rain of grace, blessing and gift."* It then rained normally.'

A leading Pharisee commented: *'What can I do with you, since even
though you importune God, he does what you wish in the same way
that a father does whatever his importuning son asks him?'*
(G. Vermes: 'Jesus the Jew' p.70)

It is in this charismatic Galilean approach to the Torah that Jesus
seems to fit best.

Glossary

Names of People

Yeshua   Jesus   Iēsous (Greek) (in Qu'ran - Isa)

The twelve disciples/trainees (based on Mark 3.16-18)

Shim'on Kefa	Simon Peter (or Simeon)
Ya'akov Bar-Zavdai	James (or Jacob) son of Zebedee
Yohanan Bar-Zavdai	John son of Zebedee
Andreas	Andrew (Greek). Simon Peter's brother
Bar-Talmai	Bartholomew - son of Ptolemy
Mattityahu	Matthew
Philippos	Philip (Greek)
Shim'on Zelotes	Simon the Zealot
T'addai	Thadaeus
T'oma	Thomas
Ya'akov Bar-Chalfai	James son of Alphaeus.
Y'hudah Ish-K'riot Bar-Shim'on	Judas Iscariot son of Simeon

Women Followers

Miryam	Mary
Marta	Martha
Shlomit	Salome
Yochana	Joanna

Friends

Zakkai	Zacchaeus
Bar-Timai	Bartimaeus
El'azar	Lazarus
Shim'on	Simon (or Simeon)

Biblical names

Avraham	Abraham
Yitzchak	Isaac
Ya'akov	James/Jacob
Moshe	Moses
Yesha'yahu	Isaiah
Yirmeyahu	Jeremiah

Jewish groups

Terms in the book	Terms in the Bible
Temple Aristocrats	Sadducees
Leading priests	Chief priests
Great Council	Sanhedrin
Council members	Elders
Torah-teachers	Scribes
Hasidim	Pharisees
Liberals	Herodians
Essenes	a quasi-monastic movement with communities in Jerusalem, Alexandria in Egypt and famously at Qumran by the Dead Sea who wrote the Dead Sea Scrolls
Judaeans	Jews

Those in Jesus' trials

Anan	Annas - short for Ananias. former High Priest
Kayafa, full name Yosef Ben-Kayafa	Caiaphas, current High Priest
Pontius Pilatus	Pontius Pilate (Latin), Procurator/Governor
Sila	Silas, priest
El'chud Bar-Nachum	Elihud son of Nahum, Temple captain

Witnesses in order of appearance

El'chud Bar-Z'kariyah	Elihud son of Zechariah
Yannai Ben-Mattat	Jannai son of Matthat
Tolmai Bar-Y'hudah	Ptolemy son of Judah
Avraham Bar-L'vi	Abraham son of Levi
Shim'on Bar-Yitzchk	Simeon son of Isaac

Places

In order of appearance

Yerushalayim	Jerusalem
Galil	Galilee/ Region
Galil ha Goyim	Galilee of the Gentiles
Natzeret	Nazareth
Yericho	Jericho
Beit-Anyah	Bethany
Beit-Pagey	Bethphage
Yisrael	Israel
Gat Sh'manim	Gethsemane
Praetorium	Governor's headquarters or Procurator's residence
Efrayim	Ephraim, modern Taybeh.
Amma'us	Emmaus

Words of Faith

Words for God and his kingdom

Elaha	God (Aramaic)
Abba	Father/Dad
Adonai	Lord - used instead of pronouncing the sacred name YHWH.
Elohim	God
Eloheynu	Our God
Elohi	My God (Hebrew)
Mar/Maran	Lord/Great Lord (Aramaic)
Ha Maschiach	The Anointed One, the Messiah, the Christ
Ruach HaKodesh	The Holy Spirit
Ben-David	Son of David (Hebrew)

Words for scripture

Torah	The law, the first five books of the Bible (Genesis to Deuteronomy)
Haftorah	The history and prophetic books of the Bible (Joshua to Malachi)
Hallel	Six psalms of praise used at Passover, Psalms 113 to 118.
The Readings	All of the Hebrew Scriptures including the Wisdom books. Later called the Tenakh - the Law, Prophets and Writings.
The Law and the Prophets	Jesus' regular term for the Jewish scriptures.
Amen	Indeed, I agree etc.

Words of worship

Shabbat	Sabbath - day of rest.
Pesach	Passover / Feast of Unleavened Bread
Nisan (called Abib in the Torah)	First month of the year, March/April
Shavuot	Feast of Weeks/Pentecost
Sivan	Third month of the year, May/June
Sukkot	Feast of Tabernacles of Booths
Mikveh	ritual bath house
Rabbi	Teacher/master
Rabban	Great teacher/master

Other Phrases

Shalom aleikhem	Peace (prosperity, well-being) to you
Tebu lak	Thank you (Aramaic). Hebrew is 'Toda'
Chutzpah	cheek, cheekiness
Ish Mavet	Man of death - sentenced to death.
Xairé	Greetings, literally Rejoice (Greek)
Aprilios	April (Greek)
Titulus	A caption, inscription or label (Latin)

Rev Andy's other books

with sample pages

Desert nomads
Ancient Egyptian wallpainting

BIBLE IN BRIEF

An easy way to explore the Bible in just six months

This book is for you if

- you are looking for an understandable way into the Bible;
- you want a clear structure arranged into six monthly topics;
- you want to choose for yourself what to read and when to read;
- you want questions to focus your responses to the readings;
- you would like to create your own Bible commentary in the book or online;
- you are curious about what other cultures of the time were saying;
- you like maps and illustrations and timelines;
- you want to end up seriously informed.

"This book does what few others do - it offers a very helpful guide for those looking for a brief overview of the Bible and its story."
Rt Revd Graham Tomlin, Bishop of Kensington

MONTH 1 WEEK 1

BEGINNINGS

Day 1 Genesis 1 + 2.1-3 The beginning of the world
Is the universe 'good'?
"Made in God's image" - what does this mean?

Day 2 Genesis 2.4-end Beginnings - another account
What do men and women need for life to be good?

Day 3 Genesis 3 Our fall from grace
What attitudes do we have that spoil life?

Day 4 Genesis 4 The first murder
What are the causes and consequences of violence?

Day 5 Genesis 6.9 - 7.end The story of the flood
Note: there were several stories of the flood in the ancient Middle East, reflecting some actual event.
How important is it that a remnant survive a catastrophe?

Day 6 Genesis 8 The end of the flood
Noah's first act on leaving the ark was to worship. Why?

Day 7 Genesis 11.1-9 Humanity disunited
Note: Babel is another name for Babylon, the empire that conquered Judah in 587 BC.
"Pride goes before a fall." Does it?

THE OTHER SIDE
STORIES FROM BABYLON

THE GILGAMESH EPIC OF THE FLOOD

The Gilgamesh Epic was composed around 2000 – 1800 BC.
Gilgamesh tries to find a way to avoid death. Finally he meets
one person to have eternal life – Uta-pishti – who obeyed they
instruction of the god Ea and survived the great flood..

"Destroy your house and build a vessel... despising possessions,
preserve what has life. Thus load in your vessel the seed of all
creatures."   Uta-pishti built a vast wooden cube, sealed with pitch,
120 cubits on each side, with six decks.

All that I had I now loaded aboard her ... silver ... gold ... yea, of the
species of all living creatures ...
all my family, kindred, beasts, wild and domestic, and all of the
craftsmen I made enter the vessel.

Swift blew the storm...
it passed over the land like a battle ...
Even the gods were afeared at the deluge, took to flight, and went
up to the heaven of Anu and cowered like dogs.

For six days and nights the wind blew,
and the flood and the storm swept the land.
But the seventh day arriving did the rainstorm subside. I opened a
vent... and I looked at the sea,
the tideway lay flat as a rooftop.
The whole of mankind had returned unto clay.

DISCOVERING PSALMS AS PRAYER

This book is for you if

- you sometimes think that prayer is a strange thing to do;
- you often don't know how to get started with prayer;
- you find the Psalms confusing (let alone the whole Bible!);
- you would like to know how to USE the Psalms in your spiritual life;
- you wonder if other churches in the world have something to teach us;
- you are interested in one person's spiritual journey in prayer.

"In Discovering Psalms as Prayer Andy Roland weaves together the wisdom of a faithful, personal pilgrimage with practical guidance for reading the psalms. It will be a gift to those wanting to make that discovery for themselves. We are in his debt."

Rev David Runcorn: Spirituality Workbook:
A Guide for Explorers, Pilgrims and Seekers;
Love Means Love etc.

From Chapter 1

The Problem of Prayer

The key problem with prayer is that we have a problem with it. As soon as we say to ourselves, *"I think I'll pray now"*, we (or at any rate, I) are/am faced with an immediate sense of reluctance. It's like starting the car and trying to drive it with the handbrake on.... So we need a strategy.

From Chapter 4

Bus-friendly Morning Prayer

The three psalms which are central to Syrian Orthodox morning prayers are psalms 51, 63 and 113.

Psalm 51 starts:
Have mercy on me, O God, according to your steadfast love;
according to your abundant mercy blot out my transgressions.

The natural ending is at verse 17:
The sacrifice acceptable to God is a broken spirit;
a broken and contrite heart, O God, you will not despise.

Psalm 63 starts:
O God, you are my God, I seek you,
my soul thirsts for you,
my flesh faints for you,
as in a dry and weary land where there is no water.

The natural ending is at verse 8:
My soul clings to you;
your right hand upholds me.

Psalm 113 starts and continues with the theme of praise:
Praise the Lord!
Praise, O servants of the Lord,
Praise the name of the Lord.

For the first time in my life I encountered psalms as prayers which made immediate sense to me. These three psalms are a wonderful ladder, leading from confession through trust to praise. I started using them daily, and found that wherever I was spiritually, something in these three psalms would speak directly to my situation. And by using them every day, I quickly got to know them by heart. Within a fortnight I could pray them anywhere without the need of a book.

My homeward journey to England started a fortnight after my visit to Kurisumala. I got an overnight coach from Madurai to Madras, a 12 hour journey, stopping every two or three hours for comfort breaks. I managed to sleep from half past midnight to 5.00. I remember looking out of the slightly leaking window at the grey rainswept countryside when I woke, praying the three psalms by memory and feeling a real connection with God.

THE BOOK OF JOB

**FOR PRIVATE READING, GROUP STUDY AND
PUBLIC PERFORMANCE + ESSAY 'THE MEANING OF JOB'**

This book is for you if

- you want to reflect on the big questions of life - suffering, injustice, faith;
- you find the Old Testament a bit unwieldy and want a straightforward way into one of the most powerful books in the Bible;
- you want a way to read Job in a week;
- you want to have a fascinating evening in a home group;
- you want to put on a public drama event, e.g. on a Sunday evening in church, to which you can invite friends and neighbours

To understand anything about how Job works, we need to hear it as drama, as an exchange of passionate, difficult speeches. Hence the importance of this 'arrangement', which allows us to enter the space of the writer's imagination and the writer's faith as it is tested, pushed and squeezed, almost rejected, revived, articulated in intense protest and equally intense trust.

Rowan Williams

Job for Group Study

Job

3: ³ 'Let the day perish on which I was born,
and the night that said,
"A man-child is conceived."
¹¹ 'Why did I not die at birth,
come forth from the womb and expire?
¹² Why were there knees to receive me,
or breasts for me to suck?
¹³ Now I would be lying down and quiet;
I would be asleep; then I would be at rest
¹⁴ with kings and counsellors of the earth,
where slaves are free from their masters.

²⁰ 'Why is light given to one in misery,
and life to the bitter in soul,
²¹ who long for death, but it does not come,
and dig for it more than for hidden treasures.

Eliphaz

4: ² 'If one ventures a word with you, will you be offended?
But who can keep from speaking?
³ See, you have instructed many;
you have strengthened the weak hands.
⁴ Your words have supported those who were stumbling,
and you have made firm the feeble knees.
⁵ But now it has come to you, and you are impatient;
it touches you, and you are dismayed.
⁶ Is not your fear of God your confidence,
and the integrity of your ways your hope?

THE MEANING OF JOB

Job

The first two chapters of the book of Job relates a series of disasters that befall Job - death and destruction caused by human wickedness; devastation of natural disasters, and finally a physical skin disease causing permanent pain and social ostracism. He has in a short space of time experienced all the worst that life can throw at us. The next 39 chapters are an impassioned debate on the meaning of life in these circumstances. But rather than exploring the problem of suffering, I believe they explore the problem of God.

The Problem of Suffering

People did, and do, ask "Why me?' "Why did this happen?" "Why do bad things happen to good people?" These are questions as widespread as the human race, and as old as history. But the writers of the Bible did not address these questions, just as Jesus did not.

At that very time there were some present who told Jesus about the Galileans whose blood Pilate had mingled with their sacrifices. He asked them, "Do you think that because these Galileans suffered in this way they were worse sinners than all other Galileans? No, I tell you; but unless you repent, you will all perish as they did."

(Luke 13:1-5)

The easiest way to explain suffering is that the people deserved it. It is the argument of Job's friends:

5 'Surely the light of the wicked is put out,
and the flame of their fire does not shine...

(Job 18.5)

259

A Greek Orthodox priest at prayer in the Church of the Holy Sepulchre

A WEEK OF PRAYER IN JERUSALEM

A TRAVELLER'S TALE
Experiencing Jerusalem in the 'Week of Prayer for Christian Unity' 2017
with over 170 colour photos

This book is for you if

* you ever wonder what it would be like to visit Jerusalem;

* you want too explore the amazing variety of churches in the holiest Christian city, and their message of peace;

* want to look behind the strident headlines and get a feel for ordinary life in Israel and the Palestinian Territories;

* are prepared to be surprised and even shocked;

* you are confused about the rights and wrongs of Israelis and Palestinians. I hope that hate book will make you more confused, but at a deeper level!

'Through his easy to read travel diary Andrew Roland gives us a colourful collage of ordinary and extraordinary encounters with Jerusalemites, places and events. Aware of conflicts and contrasts, as well as human interconnectedness, he joined the different churches celebrating the Week of Prayer for Christian Unity in the city, from where they all trace their origins.'

Rev Eliza Zikmane, Lutheran minister, City of London

MONDAY - TO BE A PILGRIM
On the Mount of Olives

I had a 20 minute walk along the ridge, passing the Makassed Islamic Charitable Hospital (250 beds) and the Princess Basma Centre for Disabled Children to reach my first stop, the Chapel of the Ascension. This is a unique piece of Jerusalem, inhabiting a sort of quiet no man's land between Christians, Muslims and latterly Jews. It is at the highest point of the Mount of Olives, 830 metres above sea level, a small octagonal courtyard which you have to pay 5 NIS to enter. The Crusaders built a charming octagonal cloister to mark the spot where Jesus ascended into heaven 40 days after his resurrection. Walls and a roof were added by Armenian Christians in 1835, turning a charming open-air plaza into a small dark chapel. In the centre, in the bare rock, is a small hollow, traditionally the footprint of Jesus as he launched himself upwards and pushed the rock which was trying to follow him back to earth. It usually has no more than couple of people inside. The leaflet says, *"Visitors come here to cherish the last spot of Jesus on earth, read passages from texts and sermons, chant and light up candles."*

The site is owned by the small mosque next door. The guide and caretaker, Mohammed, said that Christians were always welcome to pray there, and that lots came on Ascension Day. His son is a bus driver and works for an Israeli company - a fact which clearly brought him no joy.

Round the corner is one of my favourite places in Jerusalem, the Church of the Pater Noster (Our Father). Since my last visit they have started charging 10 NIS, but it is still worth it. The first church on the site was built by Constantine's mother Helena about 330 and called the Church of the Apostles, or the Church of the Olive Grove. It was destroyed by the Persians in 614. A Crusader church was built in 1152 but destroyed after Salah-ed-Din's capture of Jerusalem in 1187. Princess Aurelia Bossi bought the site in about 1860 and began searching for the cave where traditionally Jesus had taught his disciples. It has been French-owned ever since. She established a Carmelite convent and built the cloisters and church between 1868 and 1878. Between 1910 and 1915 an underground grotto and the Byzantine church were discovered and partly reconstructed.

So the place is a tranquil mix of open-air buildings and gardens, with the walls of courtyard being covered with translations of the Lord's Prayer in over 160 languages and dialects, such as Sardinian, Welsh and Cherokee. For me the centrepiece was the prayer in Aramaic and Hebrew, the actual languages of Jesus. The lush green gardens are a real oasis. I saw a small tabby cat being determinedly pursued by a three-legged tom - I assume he won. At the side of the church is a beautiful olive grove with a fantastic view over Jerusalem. I was simply sitting and enjoying the peace when sadly I was told to leave. They close the site at lunchtime, 12.00 - 2.00. In Jerusalem you have to schedule your times of peace and quiet.

Printed in Great Britain
by Amazon

20423264R00154